OPPORTUNITIES
in

Library and Information Science Careers

OPPORTUNITIES

in

Library and Information Science Careers

REVISED EDITION

KATHLEEN DE LA PEÑA MCCOOK

New York   Chicago   San Francisco   Lisbon   London   Madrid   Mexico City
Milan   New Delhi   San Juan   Seoul   Singapore   Sydney   Toronto

The *McGraw·Hill* Companies

Library of Congress Cataloging-in-Publication Data

McCook, Kathleen de la Peña.
  Opportunities in library and information science careers / by Kathleen de la Peña
McCook. —3rd ed.
      p.   cm.
  Includes bibliographical references.
  ISBN-13: 978-0-07-154531-0 (alk. paper)
  ISBN-10: 0-07-154531-X (alk. paper)
  1. Library science—Vocational guidance—United States.   2. Information
science—Vocational guidance—United States.   I. Title.

  Z682.35.V62M35   2008
  020.23'73—dc22   2008024641

1 2 3 4 5 6 7 8 9 10 11 12 13 14 15 16 17 18 19 20   DOC/DOC   0 9 8

37541850   10/08

ISBN 978-0-07-154531-0
MHID   0-07-154531-X

Interior design by Rattray Design

McGraw-Hill books are available at special quantity discounts to use as premiums and
sales promotions or for use in corporate training programs. To contact a representative,
please visit the Contact Us pages at www.mhprofessional.com.

This book is printed on acid-free paper.

Contents

PREFACE

OURS IS AN age of information. Each and every day, more and more information becomes available, and the management of this information—from its accumulation to its categorization to its storage to its dissemination—becomes more and more challenging. Imagine manipulating the data not only of days, weeks, or decades past, but of centuries—to the beginning of recorded history and beyond! The task is mammoth, yet librarians and information professionals do it all the time.

To help people get the variety of information they need quickly and easily, today's librarians and information specialists must be both knowledgeable about where and how to find the desired information and proficient in the ways of accessing it. This means that in many instances they will need prior knowledge about the information being looked for, and they will have to have the expertise necessary to locate it in whatever forms it exists, be it book, tape, microfiche, CD-ROM, journals, the Internet, and so on.

The choices are many. You can choose to be a generalist or specialist, work with children or doctoral candidates, deal with rare books or musical compilations. The disciplines in which you can work are limited only in the kind and variety of information that exists.

Because of its very nature, library and information science is a field that will continue to grow and evolve. Consequently, it will need talented, intelligent, innovative, and determined individuals to keep pace with it and to adapt to new ways of managing and organizing information. For such individuals, the rewards of this profession are great.

Acknowledgments

The authors and editors gratefully acknowledge Peggy Sullivan for her authorship and involvement in previous editions of this work and Kate Lippincott, research associate at the University of South Florida, School of Library and Information Science, for research and electronic database searching for this revision.

1

EVOLUTION OF LIBRARIES

As STEWARDS OF information, librarians and information science professionals preserve, organize, and disseminate information. Today, the ways they accomplish this vary more and more as technology, education, and information expand while the computer and communications industries grow more complex. Careers in information science and librarianship are based on skills in the organization and retrieval of recorded knowledge. Professionals design and implement systems of categorizing and classifying documents to facilitate their use.

The variety of career opportunities for the individual educated in the library and information sciences expands every day. Typical careers include the following:

- Information specialist in the petrochemical industry
- Director of a multicounty library system
- Archivist in a governmental agency or museum
- Database searcher for a nuclear regulatory agency

- Coordinator of children's services for an urban library
- Media specialist at an elementary or secondary school
- Systems analyst for a bibliographic utility
- Cataloger of classical language material at an academic library

Any work that requires organizing, analyzing, and disseminating information falls into the domain of the librarian and information scientist. Traditionally, this work has been with printed materials, but these organizational skills are increasingly being applied to electronic, visual, audio, and digital formats. In addition to assembling the material, information professionals manipulate it for diverse and specialized audiences.

Information Professionals and What They Do

The term *information professional* is broader than either *librarian* or *information scientist*: it designates individuals who have been educated to organize, retrieve, and disseminate information. This education typically consists of a bachelor's degree in the liberal arts or sciences and a master's degree in library and information science. Similar to education for law, the professional credential for information work builds upon undergraduate specialization. For example, an undergraduate degree in history or literature, coupled with the master's degree in library and information science, is ideal for public service work in an academic or public library; and an undergraduate degree in biology or chemical engineering, coupled with the master's degree in library and information science, is appropriate for technical information work in an industrial research center.

Librarians who work with young children—generally called *media specialists*—in elementary or secondary school settings may have undergraduate preparation in education or social welfare. Those who work with special language collections may have prepared by taking linguistic studies at the undergraduate level. Generally, any undergraduate study complemented with master's level work in library and information science can be tailored to a unique specialty.

Information professionals work in every kind of organization. Public institutions such as colleges and universities, public libraries, schools, and government agencies all require individuals skilled in organizing information. Corporations, advertising agencies, trade associations, and nonprofit institutions such as museums and zoos require the talents of professionals who can manage their records, retrieve data, and assemble facts for analysis.

Salaries of information professionals vary depending upon specialization, geographical region, and size and type of organization. While small public libraries may start new graduates with annual salaries in the low twenties, corporate headquarters or pharmaceutical firms often offer beginning salaries in the mid-thirties or higher. Directors of large academic libraries or technical information centers can earn more than $100,000 per year. The information professions are so diverse that broad generalizations are difficult to make. Suffice it to say that individual ability and initiative can result in salary levels comparable to those in any field. (See Chapter 4 for additional salary information.)

Careers in information science often require mobility. Most positions are advertised nationally, and advancement can take place either within one institution or from one to another. The director of information services at a medium-sized public library can become its director or move on to departmental duties at an urban library. The database searcher at an agricultural library may move on to coordinate online information services for a large system. A media specialist at a high school library may become a state consultant for media and instructional technology.

Typical affiliations with professional associations include the American Association of Law Librarians, American Library Association, American Society for Information Science, Medical Library Association, Society of American Archivists, or the Special Libraries Association. These organizations provide placement services and hold frequent conferences for continuing education.

Historical Note

The profession of library and information science has strong traditions. The discipline works with cultural records and thought and should be examined against this background. Perhaps the first individual in ancient times who had the idea of sorting, collecting, and making the Mesopotamian clay tablets or Egyptian papyrus scrolls more accessible should be recognized as the first librarian. By scanning many centuries, we can see that the status of the librarian—that is, the person responsible for maintaining a collection of information materials for use by others—rose when the need for records became recognized as important. The librarian was probably first seen as an organizer of materials—not of books as we know them today but of bulky rolls or tablets that had to be preserved if they were to be useful to others.

The Middle Ages

The value of the materials varied at different times because of their relative availability. For example, in the Middle Ages, when links with earlier cultures were few, the people concerned with records preservation attached an exceptionally great value to their work.

Today their work remains essential to our understanding of those early times, although it still has received little recognition. The determination and the development of skills for the preservation of materials remain the significant work of librarians.

Centuries before anyone dreamed of special education for librarians, it was customary for leaders of church and state to appoint a few well-read, well-organized individuals to collect materials and arrange them so that the leaders and their colleagues could find what they wanted. These individuals were probably the first people who consciously thought of themselves as librarians. In almost every Indo-European language, the words for *library* and *librarian* are closely related to those for books. In French, Danish, German, and other European languages, the root *biblio* is found in words for libraries and librarians. The same letter combination appears in ancient terms for books and in such English words as *bibliography* and *bible*. The English word *librarian* derives from the Latin word for book, *liber*. In many languages, the term designating the people who work with these materials is similar to the term for the materials themselves.

The 1600s and 1700s

In the mid-1600s, Gabriel Naudé, librarian to Cardinal Mazarin of France, wrote his now-famous book *Advice on Establishing a Library* as a practical guide for others to use in organizing collections of materials and encouraging their use. He may be considered the first known professional librarian.

Libraries became more essential as universities and colleges developed. The technological development of printing encouraged the proliferation of new works and new copies of materials, which increased the number of literate people. Librarians' subsequent gatherings in universities required the development of a way for them to share their materials and to make knowledge more readily available to students. Faculties—usually a group of scholars studying in the same general area—shared their information materials and selected someone, often one from their own group, to be responsible for this new collection. This individual consulted them about adding to the collection and offered such appropriate services as might be required. Depending on the size, tradition, and other characteristics of the university, these collections were combined into larger, more general collections. This made accessibility of the information more equitable and provided a program of general services.

The 1800s and Early 1900s

Although early libraries in the United States functioned as public libraries, they were often limited to members of a certain society or students in a Sunday school.

One of the most long-lasting benefits to public libraries was the series of grants Andrew Carnegie and the Carnegie Corporation made for public library buildings in the late 1800s and early 1900s. Each community had to promise to maintain its library, but the prospect of receiving such funds encouraged many communities to plan public library service.

Public libraries were important in the task of helping the many immigrants who came to this country in the 1800s and early 1900s to become a part of American society. There were special problems in working with people whose language and background differed from those of their neighbors, and public libraries attempted to serve them. They reached parents through their children and expanded the library's traditional schedule to provide times when the immigrants, who often worked long hours, could come to the library. Expanded collections of foreign language materials and programs that provided citizenship classes were important features of this effort.

In the last quarter of the 1800s, two developments helped change the character of libraries and librarians. A key figure in both was Melvil Dewey, who developed the Dewey Decimal Classification that is used in many libraries today. He was the vocal leader in the founding of the American Library Association and in the establishment of a formal educational program for librarians. Both of these developments were significant for the professionalization of librarianship. Librarians came to know each other through annual American Library Association conferences. Through shared experiences and formal discussions, they began to express themselves as a group on such issues as library cooperation and development, public relations, censorship, copyright policy and law, and library management.

Dewey's school, first located at Columbia College and later at Albany, New York, provided an opportunity for librarians to prepare themselves with a formal course of study. They learned classification, binding of books, and use of reference materials, as well as library history. Other schools, at universities or colleges and public libraries, were founded in the first quarter of the 1900s. Then, in response to recognition given to librarianship as a profession and the need for standardization of library education, the American Library Association recommended that library education programs be established only in institutions of higher learning.

If higher scholarship demanded access to more materials, there was no such tradition in lower-level schools until much later. *Blab schools*, so named from the practice of having children recite out loud, heavily emphasized memory usage and made little use of such scarce and expensive learning materials as books. Obviously, they were hardly places where libraries were likely to be established. Blab schools existed throughout the United States until the early 1900s.

As the twentieth century progressed, the push for libraries in elementary and secondary schools began with the recognition that high school students and faculties required organized resource materials. Once established, library use had to be encouraged, so dynamic high school libraries developed. Elementary schools have a shorter history, coming to the fore primarily after World War II. School library media specialists often came from the ranks of teachers, although the number of school libraries and the need for librarians in recent years have encouraged more people to train for this specialty as a first career. Today, most U.S. school systems employ full-time media specialists.

As the profession matured, special libraries developed. Special libraries are often associated with particular industries or businesses; but collections of special materials such as maps or special subjects such as art often form special libraries, too.

The Special Libraries Association, founded in the first decade of the 1900s, fosters the continuing education of its members and assists in development of techniques for greater service and efficiency. Special librarians are located in major population centers like Boston, Chicago, and Washington, DC, as well as in research centers, corporate headquarters, and research and development laboratories throughout the world.

Development of Information Science

The field of information science, which has grown rapidly during the past fifty years, is very closely allied to library science. The

American Society for Information Science, founded in 1937, is an association whose diverse membership continues to reflect the frontiers and horizons of the dynamic field of information science and technology.

The information profession is concerned with the ways people create, collect, organize, store, retrieve, send, analyze, and use information. The subject discipline that forms the basis for this field is called *information science*, the study of the characteristics of information and how information is transferred or handled. The field of information science emerged in the 1950s from several other disciplines, including computer science, library science, communications, business administration, mathematics, engineering, psychology, philosophy, and language arts. Information science emphasizes the application of modern technologies—joining together processes and systems, computers, satellites, and other technologies, and human resources—to provide information and information services.

Those who work to disseminate information in a variety of formats, whether they ally themselves with library associations or information associations, aim at a common goal of getting information to people who need it. What stands out about the library and information field is the diversity of the types of work and the locations in which this work is carried on.

The history of information agencies and the responsibilities of information professionals have always been closely tied to technological developments and advances. A suggestion made by the librarian at the surgeon general's office led to the development of mechanical card sorters, the predecessors of today's computers. The development of microfilm was a response to the need to store large amounts of textual information. Libraries and other information agencies were among the first large-scale users of computers, and many advances in the use and design of computer systems have come about as a result of the needs of libraries and information centers. Some of today's most challenging problems of computer programming and computer systems design are related to the needs of libraries and information systems.

Libraries Today

Today librarians and information science professionals face important, exciting challenges and a broad array of opportunities. Examining some of the key roles of the library, as identified by the American Library Association, make it is possible to gain a sense of the scope.

- **Librarians and information professionals preserve, organize, and disseminate the resources of the library so that citizens can make informed decisions.** A democracy requires the active participation of its citizenry, and libraries play a vital role in making knowledge and ideas available to everyone. The relationship of democracy and libraries is fundamental, and the stronger the library services are, the more powerful informed citizens' voices will be.
- **Libraries break down barriers.** Literacy outreach programs that teach reading, provide bilingual materials, serve the homebound, and work with the elderly continue to be a priority for librarians in order to reach segments of the population that others are failing to reach. The barriers to those who are illiterate, low-literate, and non-English-speaking are enormous, and the loss to society as a whole can have far-reaching effects.
- **Libraries level the playing field.** As the income inequities in this country grow, the library is one public institution that provides

equality of information to all. As technology and the Internet converge, the need for librarians and information professionals to provide equity to information becomes crucial.

• **Libraries value the individual.** For many authors, scientists, and politicians a librarian provided the encouragement and support needed to learn and grow. Testimonies from many successful citizens credit librarians and information professionals with opening the door to the storehouse of the world's knowledge.

• **Libraries nourish creativity.** Librarians and information professionals make it possible for learners to gain access to the books, Web pages, and digitized collections that lead to new scholarship, poetry, and scientific achievement.

• **Libraries open children's minds.** Story hours for preschoolers, stories told with wonder and magic, support for schoolwork, and individualized attention by librarians provide expansion of the world to young minds.

• **Libraries return high dividends.** Economic development for the small business and other community enterprises is found through the collaboration with librarians and other information professionals to assist in the development of business plans, the collection of data for public relations and marketing, and other crucial resources for business development.

• **Libraries build communities.** Meeting rooms at libraries provide a chance for communities to gather together and learn from one another. Librarians provide support to groups as diverse as investors and clowns. Together the community and the staff of library and information professionals help make a world where people care about each other and their future.

• **Libraries make families stronger.** Librarians support families in learning together through home schooling support, story hours, support for science projects, intergenerational reading programs, and the like.

- **Libraries make you think.** Librarians work to balance opinions and ideas within the collections they maintain. Challenges to old ways and ideas that make us think are brought together by the thoughtful work of librarians and information professionals who gather together collections for the community to read and ponder.
- **Libraries offer sanctuary.** Librarians ensure that the wise words of scholars and scientists and artists from the past are available in a manner that is accessible to all.
- **Libraries preserve the past.** Librarians sift through the onslaught of media to save and preserve our cultural heritage. In addition to its selection, preserving this heritage, whether archival or digital, is the role of the librarians.

These roles of libraries appeared in the December 1995 issue of the official journal of the American Library Association, *American Libraries.* Although these roles are timeless, their implementation will continue to change in the future.

Number of Libraries in the United States

The American Library Association estimates that there are 123,291 libraries of all kinds in the United States today. No annual survey provides statistics on all types of libraries. The counts that follow for public, academic, and school libraries come from the most recent versions of three different surveys by the National Center for Education Statistics. Figures for special libraries, armed forces libraries, and government libraries are taken from the *American Library Association Fact Sheet 1.*

Number of Public, Academic, School, and Special Libraries in the United States

Public Libraries—Administrative Units   9,198
  (Central buildings* 9,040)
  (Branches 7,503)
  (Buildings 16,543)
Academic Libraries   3,653
  (Less than four-year 1,436)
  (Four-year and above 2,217)
School Libraries   99,783
  (Public schools 82,569)
  (Private schools 17,054)
Special Libraries‡   9,181
Armed Forces Libraries   302
Government Libraries   1,174

Total   123,291

---

* The number of central buildings is different from the number of public libraries because some public library systems have no central building and some have more than one.

‡ Libraries considered "special libraries" are those with a particular focus such as corporate, law, medical, religious, and so forth.

2

Information Professionals on the Job

Where are today's information professionals working? Though more and more might exclaim "cyberspace!" the new information professionals are still likely to be affiliated with an institution. What are their institutions like? Envision a new academic library containing acres of space and rare manuscripts. Or a university's library system that includes a central library that performs many services, while a small staff manages departmental libraries. The degree of a departmental librarian's independence from the library system may vary, but the point is that both the departmental librarian and the librarian in the large central library work for the same system. Thus, while departmental librarians may exercise special skills in the management of a Slavic literature collection or a Far Eastern studies collection, they are usually tied to the central library through common governance, computer systems, and centralized processing.

Similarly, in a public library system there may be librarians in a downtown central library whose work is highly specialized in the kinds of assistance they provide to users, such as business information, literacy education, exhibits development, or humanities programming. In the same system's neighborhood branch libraries, a small staff may deal with all ages and kinds of readers and coordinate programs with community organizations and schools. However, many information professionals, especially those in corporate or research institutes, focus on the retrieval of information from databases thousands of miles away. Vendors access large databases of legal or medical information through computer terminals to search for highly discrete facts. Information professionals manipulate numeric or full-text results in raw source material for corporate planning or scientific discoveries.

Some information professionals work independently, offering their services for a fee. Others have joined the growing numbers of companies that create and market information. Additionally, thousands of companies employ information specialists to provide primary and secondary information, custom search computer and manual sources, and provide information-support services.

Health science libraries employ professionals to develop collections, educate medical staff in medical informatics, and coordinate access to electronic resources. A hospital librarian may serve as a member of a health-care team or participate in patient education.

Bookmobiles, another place of employment for information professionals, bring books to isolated locations, often in rural areas. They may also service routes that include urban shopping centers or city neighborhoods and suburbs with difficult access to other library agencies. Some school systems provide bookmobile service to small schools that cannot employ a media specialist on a regular basis.

Because bookmobiles are mobile, they are often used to demonstrate the resources of a community's library at events that reach new segments of a community, like a city arts festival or a county fair.

Special corporate libraries, located in large companies such as Motorola, Mead Data Central, or pharmaceutical groups, provide access for employees. Newspapers employ online data searchers, photo archivists, and Web masters. Museum libraries hire information professionals to organize archives, catalogs, and research collections.

A special library may occupy a suite of offices in a corporation's headquarters. It may occupy smaller areas in various regional offices, just as a library serving a sprawling research institute may have several different units located near the most relevant areas.

Legal firms and university libraries will employ astute information professionals to search multiple databases for case law and precedent.

Great strides in library cooperation have been made since the 1960s. Large regional libraries or systems employ consultant librarians who work with individual libraries in their areas to foster exchange of library materials, cooperative cataloging and acquisition, and electronic systems coordination.

Responsibilities of Information Professionals

If the locations of information employment vary so much, does the work that makes up the information professional's day differ to the same degree? Three examples suggest that the work shows even more variety. There are similarities in the kinds of responsibilities and concerns that are part of the work of three different kinds of information professionals.

Information Broker

Lee Fox and Mary Raney met while they were graduate students in an information science program and decided to set up their own "information-on-demand" business upon graduation. On a typical morning, Fox stops at a government library to peruse legal reports for a client involved in personal injury litigation, while Raney goes directly to their office to conduct a computer search of environmental regulations for a firm that is seeking a municipal permit to develop a landfill.

Their office administrator notifies them of an emergency call from a small financial counseling firm that needs a search of the ABI/Inform database to assist a new account. While the computer runs off environmental data, Raney calls up the financial database to begin that search.

When Fox returns from the library with a list of legal citations, he passes them on to their word processing operators. He then assists another client who needs marketing data by analyzing census data from Standard Metropolitan Statistical Area block statistics. Throughout the day, Lee and Mary use printed and computer sources to retrieve and compile information needed by their many clients. Initially they billed $50 per hour for services, but their client load has become so large that they now have a list of those for whom they work on a contingency basis. They greatly decrease expenses for each of these clients by using skilled information brokers rather than employing a staff specialist full-time.

Public Library Director

The public library director of one county public library with twenty-seven neighborhood branches probably begins the day with a careful, though hurried, reading of the daily newspaper. This director needs to know what the county commission candidates are promising to voters, what the prospects are for new industries, whether zoning law changes may affect residential areas and the location of branch libraries, and any other information about the county that affects the library and the public it serves.

On the national scene, the director reviews legislation relating to telecommunications and to libraries, news of controversies elsewhere about library materials, and general information about the economy. She corresponds with members of Congress on legislation relating to library funding.

Later in the morning, the director attends at least a portion of a meeting of young adult librarians. This provides an opportunity to get acquainted with staff members from outlying neighborhood branches who may come to the central library only a few times a year.

The director's other morning appointments include the library's legal counsel, who is reporting on a case instigated by an employee injured while on duty. She meets with an architect to review plans for renovation of one of the older branch libraries and later asks the human resources department to inform her about progress in filling a position that will be vacated by an important staff member who is retiring. A staff committee, working with the human resources department, has much of the responsibility for that appointment, but the director requests information about their criteria and interviewing schedule. She then participates in those interviews or schedules a separate one with some candidates, especially since the position is an important one in the library system.

Lunch, which might be a respite from the several meetings, is more likely to be an extension of them. Perhaps the director will be invited to lunch with a community organization that is requesting expansion of the Asian-language collection for new citizens or with a committee from the school board that seeks to create homework centers in partnership with neighborhood branches.

In the afternoon, she spends several hours away from the library meeting with other county department heads to consider reductions to the county's proposed budget. At this meeting she argues the need for investment in a regional cooperative library system that will benefit the county's own library system.

At the end of the working day, the director reads correspondence that includes a request to serve on the state library task force on networking, a request from a social services agency about the need for a job center at a branch library, a letter from a former colleague recommending an applicant for an open position, and a questionnaire from a federal agency about the library's services to the aging. She then dictates some answers. The end of the day finds the director heading home, briefcase full of annual departmental reports and professional journals that must be read to keep up with the latest developments in the field. That evening she attends a civic meeting where discussion is scheduled on a new facility that would serve as community clinic, day-care center, and library. These are just a few of her many responsibilities.

University Library Director

The day of a library director at a university has some similarities to that of the public library director. This director, too, needs to know the current concerns of the public, to meet with university vice presidents and deans to discuss the budget, to be alert to various specialists' interests on the library staff, and to deal with a range of problems relating to the need for more storage space, new copyright laws, the cost of electronic reference services, and so on.

The academic library director's correspondence may be similar to the public library director's in amount and kind. The social obligations—perhaps attending a lecture by a professor of comparative literature who has just donated valuable manuscripts to the library's special collections—have similarities.

Since scholarship is often an important aspect of academic librarianship, the director may spend an hour developing notes for a journal article about the cost-effectiveness of computerized acquisitions systems or evaluating the publication record of a staff member who is being considered for promotion.

Both directors probably started out in librarianship thinking that they wanted to work with books and with people. But at the administrative level, these professionals primarily organize, plan, and represent their institutions.

Specialization of Work by Type of Institution

Though many categories of institutions may be discussed, the main ones are public libraries, special libraries, academic libraries, school library media centers, and other information agencies. Each category contains positions that are quite similar to positions elsewhere, meaning that an individual may move without difficulty from one type to another.

Public Libraries

Probably most familiar are public libraries. These libraries are supported by public monies that come from the local community, county, state, federal government, or some mix of these agencies. Though private funds such as endowments may supplement the funding, public libraries are often closely tied to the economic situation of government support. Another major characteristic is that their programs and priorities usually are based on the general needs of the public as a whole.

In structure, it is more and more common for public libraries to be linked with others in some administrative pattern. Some systems stem from a strong central library that provides services to numerous smaller branch libraries. Others are composed of a number of independent or fairly independent libraries that have combined to share resources more effectively but that have considerable administrative freedom. Since the nature of the structure has considerable effect on the individual working in any one of the libraries, it is a good idea for any prospective employee to learn about the structure before applying for, and certainly before accepting, a position in a public library.

Public library services may extend considerably beyond the public library buildings. The public library often services and/or provides bookmobile service to jails, retirement homes, institutions for the mentally ill, and other similar places on a regular basis or through special programs.

Special Libraries and Information Centers

Often subdivided into many categories, special libraries and information centers might include medical, legal, hospital, commercial, and industrial categories. Their audience is usually carefully defined—the research staff of a chemical corporation, scholars who wish to use the library of a museum or art gallery, or patients of a hospital, for example. An important distinction should be made between medical and hospital libraries. The former are usually comprised of special collections of medical books and other media required by researchers and practitioners in a hospital, medical school, or similar institution; the latter are more like general libraries in the scope of their collections and are used by hospital patients, staff, and visitors. Medical librarians need background and information about medicine as a field of study. Hospital librarians provide more general materials, so that while information about various patients' attitudes and disabilities may be useful, they do not always need the specific background in medical sources.

There is a growing trend for agencies with special libraries in various branch offices or regional headquarters to build them into networks for greater efficiency. Thus, a producer of agricultural equipment may have a library at its main Midwestern plant that includes materials on engineering, patents, and aspects of production and inventory control, while another information center in its corporate headquarters provides information about marketing, advertising, legal questions, and other matters that concern that staff. Yet it may be useful for each library to know about the work and the content of the other. This trend often results in computerized data banks, electronic communication, or exchange of personnel. Therefore, special libraries that may appear small in some aspects, in reality offer great diversity of experience and complexity of management.

Special libraries, which are not usually tied directly to the public economy, may offer more prospect of expansion than other kinds of libraries. The services that special library staffs provide their clientele, such as journal routing in specialized fields, new publications' and productions' awareness services, clipping services, quick reference, abstracts, Web pages, or bibliographic searches offer suggestions for those interested in developing valuable freelance library and information services. In many instances, it is hard to draw a sharp line between special librarians and information scientists. Even more than other librarians, special librarians often provide a direct link with the information sought, eliminating the need to refer the requester to another library or information agency. As noted earlier, they are likely to have a close link of interest and competence with the subject field. Law libraries, for example, are often headed by lawyers who later became librarians or by librarians who have some legal knowledge.

Academic Libraries

All accredited institutions of higher education in the United States have libraries. The library, since it exists to serve the goals of the institution, may be highly oriented to research or more directed to the information needs of students or some combination of the two. In the 1960s, major growth in the establishment of community colleges included development of library programs that incorporated many kinds of media. They were usually planned with the needs of the adult learner in mind and provided extended hours and locations of service to accommodate the schedules and sprawling campuses of the institutions.

Library programs in four-year colleges range in diversity as much as the colleges do in their programs, locations, and goals. While these libraries may be small, in recent years the recognized value of cooperation among libraries has led many to form formal or informal networks to make interlibrary loans, union lists of serials, and collection development more efficient.

University libraries tend to be more concerned with research than other academic libraries. This means that acquiring and pro-

viding access to a large and richly varied collection of library materials are of great importance. The services they provide to students,
faculty members, and researchers call for library personnel who
have enough knowledge of subject areas in which advanced degrees
are offered.

Academic librarians are often involved with teaching. Government reports on education have underscored the need for Americans to become adept at information use. Academic librarians
specialize in classes that teach skills to students at all levels. Many
academic libraries hold faculty seminars and student seminars in
the use of information resources, often focusing on electronic
access.

Academic libraries, especially those serving large universities, are
the repositories of many rare and specialized collections. Work in
these collections may require extensive and specialized subject
expertise on the part of employees. Government documents from
Southeast Asia, oral histories of Native Americans, manuscript collections of public officials, and rare art prints and engravings are
just a few of the types of materials collected in academic libraries
that employ subject experts.

School Library Media Centers

On the whole, the development of school library media centers in
the United States is relatively recent. Earlier service to schools from
state education agencies or from public libraries has yielded to provisions for media centers within each school. In most school systems, the tradition of library service is usually older at the secondary
level than at the elementary level. Both levels usually emphasize
provision of materials and services that are closely related to the
school's curriculum. In recent years, the move toward provision of

a range of instructional technology, CD-ROM, and hypermedia—films, videotapes, recordings, and graphic materials—has been strong in school library media centers. Today, Internet access and the provision of computers make media specialists among the most technically expert in school systems.

The close relation of the school library media center to the curriculum usually results in the media specialist actually teaching, especially in the areas of research and use of instructional technology. As teaching information retrieval skills is a central responsibility, there are many occasions when the school library media specialist conducts classes. Media personnel are expected to have teaching skills. Most who enter this specialization have come from the ranks of teachers.

School system library services may be more complex than those of public libraries, with technical services, networking and instructional technology, film loans, professional libraries for teachers, and other related services offered by system headquarters. Supervisors of such programs may evaluate the work of media specialists in individual schools as well as be responsible for providing services from the system.

It would be misleading to leave the impression that all school library media centers are in public schools and that all are parts of systems. Private, parochial, and other nonpublic schools share many characteristics of the school library media centers described, but each school tends to be more independent in setting its own program and priorities than is a public school within a system. These schools are less likely to have such specific requirements for personnel certification.

Certification is usually required of all teaching and administrative personnel in school systems. Librarians and media specialists may be required to hold certification in those specialties and to have certification as teachers. Since certification is administered by state education agencies, requirements vary from one state to another; however, some common patterns emerge. Academic work in education, with courses in teaching methods, psychology, the organization of schools, and related subjects, is usually a requirement. The individual is typically expected to provide some evidence of competence, either as a student teacher, media intern, or perhaps as a regularly employed teacher or librarian. This shows the individual has worked well in a situation similar to the one for which he or she will receive a certificate.

Many states have made reciprocity agreements to accept each other's certificates. This is due to problems that result for individuals who move from one state to another and need to fulfill differing requirements and because of the problems of administering certification programs. Many states have made reciprocity agreements to accept each other's certificates. A person with a teaching, library, or media certificate in one state may be eligible for certification in another state simply by presenting proof of previous certification. No assumptions should be made about certification, however, because programs change. It is important to realize the significance of employment certification in a school system and to take action to achieve it.

Other Information Agencies

So far we have discussed library and information employment along the lines of four major categories of institutions: public libraries, special libraries, academic libraries, and school library media centers. The previous examples of information brokers show that some professionals in this field are not tied to specific institutions in order to earn a living.

Many government agencies at the federal, state, or international level require the services of information professionals or consultants. The U.S. Congress or a state legislature, for instance, needs analysis of laws and precedents for its deliberations on public policy; an information analysis center, such as the Oak Ridge National Laboratory, requires organization of research, reports, regulations, and environmental impact studies; a national opinion research center must have its data tapes stored and organized for access. These varied agencies employ individuals who are competent in organization skills. As the nation's output of information steadily increases, professional positions will expand in such areas.

Specialization by Professional Function

Though many information professionals can characterize their work by type of institution—such as *academic librarians* or *information institute analysts*—many types of positions exist in each institution. We will describe some of the primary functional job types to demonstrate the kinds of work that information professionals do within institutions that serve different publics.

Public Service

Providing service to a public is the object of most information-related work, though that public may be defined in different ways. Two challenges attract people to public service in the information profession: the search for information and the need to assist a public that may or may not know or be able to express what it wants. Yet even they—the children's librarian who has a lively preschool story hour in the morning and a hectic two hours of reference assistance in the afternoon; the reference librarian who divides his or

her time between assisting patrons at the online catalog and working at the telephone information desk; the bookmobile librarian
who stands while assisting eager users at two three-hour stops during the day—have behind-the-scenes work that must be done. The
children's librarian must prepare a budget to rebind the many books
that were new when the library opened and as a result, have all worn
out at the same time. The reference librarian needs to scan review
journals to select items for purchase, and the bookmobile librarian
may spend time between stops catching up on the work of choosing new books. These are only a few of the tasks they perform, yet
each of them is classified as a public service librarian. The following pages discuss varieties of public service work.

Information Services

There are several levels of information service provided in libraries
and related agencies. These include "ready reference," often by telephone or e-mail; basic assistance in answering complicated questions requiring several sources; and in-depth assistance.

Ready-reference queries include such questions as: "Who won
the 2000 Nobel Peace Prize?" "What are the major novels of the
author Manlio Argueta?" "Is the boiling point of mercury higher
than that of bauxite?" "How many votes did Bill Clinton receive
the second time he ran for president?" Academic, public, or community college librarians who provide this service may use common reference sources such as almanacs or encyclopedias to
respond, but today they increasingly turn to electronic reference
tools or the Internet.

The second level of information assistance may require several
sources for an adequate answer. Examples include such questions
as: "Can you help me identify key arguments on the abortion

issue?" or "How have architects integrated ideas from modern art into their building facades?"

In research libraries or special libraries serving a demanding clientele, information professionals do more than advise on answers or sources. They execute online computer searches, retrieve cited documents, and even analyze their contents. At a law library, for instance, a legal scholar may need to prepare a paper on the validity of the pay equity argument. In response to this need, the law librarian may search databases such as LEXIS, then copy relevant citations from microformatted sources, and finally prepare a legislative history of pertinent laws.

In a health sciences library, the medical librarian asked to assist a surgeon on a cancer case will most likely search CANCERLIT online, MEDLARS, or even EIS (Digest of Environmental Impact Statements) to collect all relevant documents. Online searching provides quick and comprehensive data for the skilled searcher to apply to the problem at hand.

Closely allied to information services is the interlibrary or cooperative function. The capacity to search hundreds of electronic databases for bibliographic citations or full text creates a greater demand for the original sources. If the library does not hold these sources, then the information services librarian must access a computerized or manual listing of the serial or monographic holdings of other research collections to initiate document retrieval.

Information and Referral Services

Closely allied to information services is the information and referral (I&R) function. I&R centers, usually housed in public libraries or governmental agencies, put people together with resources that meet their needs for survival. An unemployed laborer whose child is in need of diabetic counseling can contact the I&R service to discover if there are any publicly provided health-counseling clinics. A retired grocer whose Social Security check has been stolen can contact the I&R service for information on the correct course of action. I&R professionals often have undergraduate preparation in social welfare in addition to graduate study in library and information science.

Readers' Services

There is no single good term for the kinds of assistance provided in general readers' services. In the 1940s, public libraries placed heavy emphasis on the guidance of readers, suggesting individually designed reading programs for enjoyment or educational value. Librarians who provided this kind of service were usually called *readers' advisers*. The term is used less often today, but the service itself continues and, in some libraries, has expanded considerably. Though some libraries have continued the more personalized service, many others provide as much assistance as possible through "floor work" by staff members. Conversational guidance and assistance may be conducted in an informal way, but the purpose usually is to provide as much assistance as is available and useful to the library patron.

Many of a library's services result from observations made by those providing readers' services. Repeated inquiries about income tax information, for example, may make it clear that the collection on that topic needs to be considerably expanded or that a series of talks by accountants or representatives of the Internal Revenue Service would be a worthwhile public service for the library to provide. If many users seem unable to locate what they want on their own, the observant librarian who provides readers' services in an academic library may realize the need to start a program of library skills instruction. Though most readers' services work involves direct communication with the public, the work can be effectively extended through many other channels, such as providing bulletin boards for events within the school, college, or community. Other exhibits designed to increase public awareness of the library's services and programs, such as a local history corner to point out extensive genealogical resources, are a logical part of the service provided to readers.

Special Categories Services

These types of services usually have developed from a library's readers' services programs. For example, categories by age are common enough in public libraries. Service to children probably has the longest tradition in this country. In recent years, service to the aging has been recognized as an important area. Knowing what materials are available as well as understanding the particular characteristics of each age group is necessary to fully serve these groups. But even understanding is not enough; your respect for the individual, in spite of the possible discipline problems that children may create or the querulousness of the senile, is essential.

Special librarians, including those in public or academic libraries' science and technology departments, have a public selected for them. At least this is true to some extent, since their collections attract a certain kind of user. This applies to other specialties, as well; for example, when the homebound people in a community request library service through one librarian, who conducts an active telephone service and schedules deliveries by volunteers or other staff members. Service to the blind and people with other disabilities may be specifically assigned to one person or to a team whose skills are appropriate to that work.

Many additional examples of public service specialization for certain groups exist. In large urban areas, librarians with fluency in the dominant languages of various ethnic communities may be in demand to provide public services or to tell stories to children. Prison library service usually requires an individual with some social service background who has skills in coping with the special problems of those who are institutionalized. Librarians in rural county libraries best serve their agricultural publics if they have some background in the information needs of the farming community. Information professionals who choose to work with these specific types of publics usually supplement their general library skills with continuing education so as to provide better service, unless they have a previous background in that particular field.

Other Aspects of Public Services

It should be clear from this discussion that a number of kinds of public service exist. Some cut across other categories to include public service as part of their responsibilities. Additionally, many members of library and information center staffs think of their work or specialization as being a certain subject (art or chemistry) or a format or media (films or musical recordings). They are actually important members of the public service staff, as are the bookmobile staff members and those who provide service to the homebound, give book talks or storytelling programs in schools or at camps, or are on call or provide programs for adult service clubs and similar groups.

Technical Services

The effectiveness of public service personnel is no better than the quality of work that makes their service possible. To cite an obvious example, it would be ineffective for a museum's librarian to offer to display books available for Christmas purchases if the books had not been ordered, organized, or cataloged, and delivered to the museum library's exhibition cases for display.

Librarians who make these services possible usually are described as *technical services personnel*. The once-distinct lines between public and technical librarians have blurred as a result of the increasing complexity of the types of materials published and the changing technologies used to catalog and classify material. In the largest sense, technical services librarians provide a great deal of public service. Descriptions of the types of technical services follow.

Acquisitions

Responsibility for deciding which items a library will purchase, the agent from whom they will be purchased (an increasingly complex task as vendors of books computerize their operations), and how the library will coordinate all the suggestions it receives about purchases lies with the librarians in acquisitions work. Such work may require extremely specialized knowledge about the book trade, especially when foreign materials make up a sizable portion of the collection, as well as a keen understanding of the public for whom the materials are selected. The librarian who acquires college-level materials for a community with a low reading level fails to respond adequately to that community. It is vital for the acquisitions librarian to learn as much as possible about the local constituency before ordering material for the library at hand.

Prior to ordering material, the acquisitions librarian often reads several reviews of a single item from a variety of professional journals to ascertain the item's value to the library. Careful records must be kept to avoid duplication and to ensure that enough information exists for efficient cataloging and classification of items to be added to the collection. Today, computerized systems that maintain machine-readable files of a given library's holdings do much of the acquisitions work. Vendors can be notified of new orders via telecommunications. Skill in the use of these automated systems is now fundamental to the acquisitions process.

Many libraries now are hiring *collection development librarians* or *collection management librarians* to provide oversight in shaping and building the collection and in directing the growth of the collection to meet the needs of the library's public.

Cataloging

This is the process of describing library material so that users will know if they wish to see it. Most libraries employ computerized catalogs that let users search by author, title, subject, or keyword. Unless we use libraries in some sophisticated way or for some particular purpose, we may not realize all the decisions necessary to make the catalog as useful as possible. A cataloger needs to make decisions based on a range of questions, such as the following:

- Are people more likely to look for Victoria Holt's books under that name or under one of the same writer's several pseudonyms? For example, will users want to know that this writer is also Jean Plaidy?
- Since studies show that most university students want the most recent title on a subject, should we consider rearranging much of our catalog, with the titles that are on the same subject arranged by publication date, rather than by author?
- Is acupuncture so significant—and do we have enough books on the topic—that it requires a subject heading?

- Will third-graders be able to find books on the sea if the heading for them is "oceanography"? If not, what shall we file these books under?
- In a set of four filmstrips, is it important for the user to know the title of each, or is the title of the set enough?
- If we have a backlog of materials to be cataloged, how can we decide which groups of materials should have priority?

Of course, the list of questions could be much longer, but the point is to suggest the range of the cataloger's concerns and to indicate how closely they are related to those of public service librarians and to the library's users. It is clear that the cataloger's decisions involve other members of the library staff, including the budget officer and administrators, who must decide whether or not such decisions are feasible.

Because catalogers deal primarily with the library's materials, they may need such skills as special knowledge in various subject areas, reading knowledge of one or more foreign languages, and the ability to skim reading materials rapidly to decide how they should be organized. Skills relating to nonprint materials such as films, recordings, photographic slides, or videotapes and computer software may require knowledge of music, the ability to identify artists and composers when their names do not appear on the material, and a variety of other abilities. Within this cataloging specialty there may be many other specializations, such as music, law, serials, and government documents; large collections require adept handling of the many special items that are part of the library. And while a sense of how the readers will use a collection is important for catalogers to have, their decisions are often made in isolation, without opportunity to refer to the practices in other libraries or to ask for several options. Competence and self-assurance are vital to their judgments. There is something fascinating about sorting and putting together similar things and separating different things. Catalogers thrive on that fascination.

Cataloging information comes from a number of different sources. These include the Library of Congress, networks or consortia such as the Online Computer Library Center, the Research Libraries Information Network, and the Western Library Network.

Cataloging data from external sources makes it possible for libraries to assign many cataloging tasks to support staff; however, there is always some need for original cataloging. Professional catalogers generally catalog items for which no external sources of data are available and supervise the activities of support staff.

Cataloging requires the ability to rapidly understand the general theme and content of the material to be cataloged. Attention to detail, an important characteristic of catalogers, requires that they verify large quantities of information and make the material they are adding to the library's collection as accessible as possible. Is the book really a second edition? Does the library already have a copy of the recording? How can the discussion guide that accompanies a film be made as accessible as the film? These questions are important to consider and answer.

Intellectual ability, possibly including the ability to read several foreign languages, is an important quality for a cataloger. Assigning a classification number, often the only task an outsider is aware of, may be the smallest and least important part of the cataloger's duties.

The constant exercise of judgment and understanding of what characteristics may be traded off for others in the whole area of technical services are necessary abilities. For example, is it so important to get large quantities of seasonal materials to the patrons that the materials can be processed with only a minimal amount of cataloging information noted? Should paperback books on various careers be prepared so that they can be filed in a vertical file by subject rather than listed in a card catalog by author, title, and subject? Should terms that have become dated or misleading because of changed usage be dropped as subject headings—"Science Fiction" replacing "Interplanetary Voyages—Fiction," for instance? If so, should all earlier items have their headings changed? These examples merely suggest the responsibilities of the cataloger, which are usually shared with the head of technical services.

Other Technical Processes

The behind-the-scenes processing of library materials does not end with the cataloging and classification of materials. A wide variety of other processing activities must take place; materials must be marked for proper placement within the collection. The process of preparing materials for circulation may require preparing the materials themselves, then preparing records for a manual or automated circulation system. Many materials require special treatment: audiovisual media, computer software, archival materials, pamphlets, and rare books all must be handled with special care. Though the processes themselves may be routine, the decisions made regarding those processes require careful professional attention. New methods and techniques must be developed and instituted as changes take place in needs and materials. Technical services librarians are often on the cutting edge of library technology.

Technical services may include provision of such processes as mending materials, binding, and the referral of some items to an outside agency for repair. For instance, a film department might attach its own leader (a blank strip similar to the film itself used at the beginning of the film, sometimes with a notation as to the title and owner of the copy), or this chore may be a part of technical services. Reinforcing paperbacks within the technical services department may prove to be more economical than paying the increased price to have them reinforced by the supplier. And it may make a lot of sense for the technical services staff to be responsible for gathering up all serials and journals to be bound, keeping a record of what is sent, and handling all the physical aspects of that work.

In fact, with many libraries spending an increasing amount of their resources on periodicals and journals, along with the growing numbers of these available items, periodicals or serials work is becoming a specialty in technical processes. Preservation activities are of increasing importance to protect and prolong the life of the collection.

Library and Information System Automation

Some of the first practical uses of computers were made in libraries, and automation has had a pervasive effect on the information professions. Computers are used for everything from teaching tools in school library media centers to computer-managed archives in corporate information centers to huge systems of multidisciplinary databases provided by search service vendors.

Though automation was at first limited to large institutions with substantial budgets, advancing technology has made the adoption of computer technology feasible even for small public and school libraries. This has had two major effects on information professionals. First, an understanding of automation systems and networking has become a fundamental requirement; any information professional must have at the minimum a basic knowledge of the ways in which computers operate and the tasks that automation can accomplish.

Second, there is a growing need for information professionals who are automation experts. The automation needs of libraries and similar information institutions are inherently different from those of stores, manufacturers, and other businesses. Frequently the bodies of data that need to be manipulated are large and complex, and they must be tailored to meet varied and complex information needs. Effectively planning, designing, and implementing an automated information system is a difficult task requiring special skills. The information professionals who undertake such activities may have any number of titles: *systems analyst, library automation specialist,* and *database manager,* for example. These professionals are required to have a thorough understanding of the needs of information agencies and the ways in which computer technology can meet those needs.

Administration

We have already described a typical day in the life of a public and academic library director. The work of the administrator in the information professions closely parallels the work of any administrator in the public sector. The central concern for administrators is planning—planning to ensure that the information institution they direct continually develops services to meet the needs of the community it serves. In large libraries, planning and public relations often take up most of the administrator's time. In smaller institutions, personnel and budgeting come under the purview of the administrator as well.

Most administrators have come up through the ranks. This first-hand knowledge of how a library works allows them to mentor others within the system. Those with administrative responsibilities often take on policy-making positions within the state or national library and information associations. They work not only to develop services in their own institutions but also to enhance the quality of information provision in general.

A wide range of administrative positions exists in the information professions. The director of a corporate information center may have a small, highly trained, computer-oriented staff that works with a specialized subject matter. For example, management of an advertising firm's information center might focus on several large client accounts that deal with processed dairy products or soybean derivatives. Or perhaps the director of a large urban library may manage a central facility housing more than a million volumes and dozens of branch locations—an operation employing hundreds of people.

The manager of any information agency, regardless of its size, must be flexible, adaptable, and knowledgeable about the rapidly changing technologies used to efficiently provide information and the materials that contain it. Effective administrators must be well versed in both the public and technical service aspects of institution management and have strong people skills.

Specialization by Type of Material

The focus of some information professionals is defined by the type of material with which they work. *Data librarians* organize large collections of data for analysis and must devise special routines for storing, formatting, and retrieving data from CD-ROMs. *Photog-*

raphy librarians catalog their collections with special attention to scale and size. They develop retrieval systems that permit the comparison of different techniques. *Music librarians* provide analytic entries to their collections that take into account both composers and performers.

One of the most common of these specialties would be the *film* or *videotape librarian*, who selects films and videotapes for purchase, plans programs with other library colleagues as well as with the general public, and encourages good use of the library's collection of films, videotapes, and other nonprint media.

Most libraries in schools and community colleges have moved rapidly in the development of collections that include a wide variety of nonprint media. In these cases, librarians' responsibilities include more than working with nonprint materials. Assignment is divided according to the type of material. This can be seen in school districts where a school library media specialist has responsibility for all professional materials being used by teachers. Perhaps he or she handles the collection of curriculum materials gathered from within the district and from other parts of the country.

Another kind of specialty by type of material is that of the *map librarian*. Federal libraries, academic libraries, public libraries, and special libraries may all have map librarians on staff who interpret and organize map collections. Because of the practical problems of handling odd-sized maps and globes, this is a specialization that requires appropriate background in academic areas that are related to geography.

The same principles hold true for *government information librarians*. Their responsibilities may include not only United States documents, but those from such agencies as the United Nations and state and local governments as well. These documents may be integrated into a library's general collection, or they may be housed separately so that users can find all government documents in one place. Government information is increasingly available on the Internet. The formats of government documents vary, but this is another instance where the origin of the material determines the specialty to which it is assigned.

Production of Media

Production of media has become of increasing importance in all types of information centers. In more sophisticated systems, this includes the use of hypermedia, live and taped television productions, preparation of graphics, and individualized computer-assisted instruction software. Demand for these more sophisticated media requires staff members with special skills in production and design of exhibits and with graphic talent and ability.

Cable television has opened up new responsibilities for the information professional assigned to media production. In many cities, the public library has been designated its own cable channel. As this trend continues, media skills will become more important to the library that wants to provide a full range of service to its public.

Like technical services, these production services require that the personnel know how the materials will be used. These personnel responsibilities may be associated with a public service or public relations department, or they may be considered an adjunct of technical services or of the general media program.

Information Science

Some information science positions are filled by librarians. The training for both types of professionals is generally through a school of library and information science. The two fields are closely allied.

The American Society for Information Science describes four major categories of positions in the information science field.

Operation of Information Systems

Abstractor-indexers process the intellectual content of documents for convenient retrieval, usually through online terminals operated by *bibliographic searchers*. These searchers may work full-time at keyboard terminals or may double as *information services librarians*. As demand for services in this area grows, most larger public libraries and many academic libraries will find it important to employ individuals with these skills. Most special libraries serving business or industry already employ specialists in computerized bibliographic searching.

Database managers analyze, manipulate, and coordinate raw data in numeric format for efficient use by researchers and management. This may mean the systematization of a company's production records or implementation of large data sets of survey data for social research use by the company. *Electronic resources librarians* manage the databases that libraries license from third-party vendors.

Microform technologists use a wide range of sophisticated equipment to miniaturize or reproduce documents of other records. They work closely with publishers and computer specialists to develop new services that may never be presented in paper format.

Management of Information Systems

Many personnel often report to a single manager who coordinates information services, records management, information storage and retrieval, and consulting on communication flow. The information systems manager sometimes oversees the development of broader services, such as national networks of specialized information.

Design of Information Systems

Applications or *systems programmers* write large-scale computer programs to solve information problems in fields such as business, science, and education. *Information consultants* advise management of marketing strategy or business expansion through information systems. *Management information systems specialists* meet the information needs of decision makers through automated systems that they design and implement.

Research and Teaching

Computational linguists analyze word and language structures to determine how the computer can manipulate text for editing, indexing, classifying, abstracting, searching, or retrieving. *Cyberneticists* study the communication and manipulation of information and its use in controlling the behavior of biological, physical, and chemical systems. Teaching in all the areas outlined as information science usually includes basic research on the phenomena of information.

Positions in information science are found in libraries, data-processing centers, industry, and government. The growth of the importance of information means that new careers are being generated all the time. Education in library and information science provides the ideal preparation for this burgeoning field.

Opportunities for Information Professionals in Other Settings

Just as it is true that not everyone who works in an information institution such as a library is a librarian, not all librarians work in libraries. Because librarians often come from other academic fields with advanced academic backgrounds, they have opportunities to combine their information skills with those backgrounds; such combinations may lead them away from positions in libraries. They may develop new specialties that make positions outside library settings available to them.

Archives

Many librarians and information scientists have taken on the responsibilities for the archives of their educational institutions. As the work of that area has increased and these professionals have developed expertise in archival work—either through experience, further education, or a combination of the two—they have chosen to become *archivists*. The work requires many of the same competencies that librarianship requires. Though such vocational shifts may be made gradually over several years, the result is that a person who began work as a librarian has moved into another professional area.

The archivist works with acquisitions—the organization and use of materials, records, and other items. Acquisitions sometimes requires active searching for materials among the papers of individuals or in the bulky records of an institution. It can include the organization and use of manuscript materials. Records may include personnel records, ledgers, or promotional materials. Other items can be as varied as an executive's desk set or the time capsule placed in the cornerstone of a corporation's new building. The purpose is preservation of the historical record of the association, movement, or corporation. It should be clearly understood that not all archivists are librarians but that this is a specialization into which many librarians have successfully moved.

Publishing

Librarians or information specialists work in specialized areas, such as editorial work and other positions in the general area of publishing. Several professional journals serve librarianship and information science, and their staff members often have had education and experience in those specialties. Though such positions are few, the individuals who hold them can move on to more general editorial responsibilities in book publishing that are often related to the library and information fields. Attention to details, the ability to sense the needs of users who want reference materials, and the desire to provide for those needs are typical characteristics that information professionals share with the editors of such reference aids as indexes, abstracting services, and directories. Thus, many librarians have become valued members of such staffs. In administrative posts of publishing firms, some former librarians, who typically began their publishing activities by advising publishers about the needs of the library, have found interesting positions that are important for the library and information fields.

Some organizations, such as publishers, seek librarians with sound knowledge of a particular market to promote materials to libraries. Some general trade publishers, for example, maintain departments of school and library promotion, where the personnel need to know what kinds of announcements, catalogs, and other publicity techniques will be most appealing to the large library market. In many cases they maintain close communication with some members of the library profession who play important roles in the selection of materials. Sometimes the value of having been a former library colleague may be quite significant, and many of the people in school and library promotion have come from the library field.

The close link between librarians who work with children and the staff members of juvenile departments of trade publishers is based on an interesting history. In the early years of this century, children's librarians became more and more interested in encouraging the publication of good children's books. When separate departments for children's books were established, it was natural that children's librarians would fill many of those posts. Though this is still true today, people from a variety of backgrounds are now also filling these positions.

One part of editorial work and writing in which librarians continue to be prominent is that of reviewing. In many libraries, librarians prepare short, readable, evaluative notes on books and other materials. In these they comment briefly on the content, compare the new item with others available, and note its value in terms of its format, price, and availability. These same skills are important for journals that publish large numbers of reviews. Where staff members do the writing, their members may come from the ranks of librarians; when the journal relies on outside reviewers, a large number of them may be librarians who did this as a professional service or for a fee.

Multimedia

As the scope of the material resources available to libraries has broadened, some librarians have moved into positions of new responsibility that reflect that expansion. For example, administrative reasons might make it desirable to have one person responsible for all aspects of materials in a community college. Perhaps, the former director of the library becomes the administrator for the entire educational media program, with responsibilities for television production as well as utilization of all other media. Next the administrator moves to an administrative post with responsibility for the operation of the bookstore or for other curricular areas. This could include administration of the educational program for library technical assistants. Competence, interest in a diversity of fields, and willingness to take some risks in achieving goals are the determining factors to expand one's career.

Information Brokering

Recently, librarians have been forming agencies or companies of their own to provide information service to industries, writers, or other groups that require this type of work. While librarians may do this individually, working in groups of two or more allows them to function as a team when they have a heavy workload. This allows them to use individual skills and knowledge more effectively. They may choose genealogical searching, long a province for freelancers, but they may verify citations for writers, gather a number of references (for someone who knows in general what he or she wants but does not have the time to find and organize it), and read and prepare notes on reference materials for others.

Information Consulting

Information scientists may choose the same kinds of freelance work. Special competencies include bibliographic searching of online information systems, preparation of technical reports as editors or writers, or preparation of large-scale computer programs for information storage and retrieval. These specializations, as well as librarianship, offer the opportunity for people to work as consultants. They may advise on major purchases or selections of systems, make recommendations of building projects, conduct initial searches and interviews for major personnel appointments, advise on the development of media collections, or provide—on a fee basis—their expertise in some other area requiring research.

Usually consultants of this kind have been recognized for their competence because of their previous work in regular full-time positions. The good decisions made by a library administrator during the planning and construction of a new library, for instance, may cause another administrator to invite him or her to serve as a consultant in another building program; or the reputation that a bibliographer develops in selecting materials for the library where he or she works may result in another library's seeking that bibliographer's assistance when considering major purchases in areas with which its own staff may be less familiar.

Because consultants' work is almost always based on extensive experience, and because employment possibilities are difficult to predict in this kind of work, it is a specialty that information professionals often practice when they retire from full-time work. Being able to combine retirement with work that supplements income and provides a change of scene and experience is an appealing prospect to many retirees.

Perhaps another word might be said here about consultants. When library personnel see a consultant come into a library in the morning, perhaps fresh from the airport and carrying a suitcase, then see the consultant leave at the end of the day, evidently off to a new assignment, library personnel may characterize the work as glamorous. They may be critical when they see the budget item for the consultant's work. They are probably not aware, however, of the extensive study the consultant may do in advance of each visit and the high pressure and tension under which he or she may have to work while on the scene. They may not consider the amount of time needed to prepare and present a report on the consultant's findings, either. Such reports may go to a board of trustees or a general administrator rather than to the library's own administrator, and they are certain to prompt questions the consultant must be prepared to answer. Major components of consulting work include professional knowledge, personal confidence, common sense, experience, the ability to think on one's feet, and the willingness to acknowledge errors. As previously mentioned, individuals who work their way into such positions have usually done so after long years in other kinds of responsible supervisory or administrative work.

Professional Association Work

In addition to self-employed library and information specialists, there are others who work in neither libraries nor information centers but nonetheless need a thorough knowledge of their field. For example, librarians serving as consultants or representatives often fill staff positions in the various national library and information associations. In staff positions they might work as association managers with other professional people, travel extensively to conferences, prepare promotional materials for their associations, and handle many other tasks that need to be done when officers of such associations have only limited time for their responsibilities. Because many librarians often have had on-the-job experience with similar responsibilities, they are good choices for such posts.

A growing number of state and regional library and information associations employ staff persons. Though not all of these are information professionals, they often come from the ranks of library employees because they need to be familiar with the work of their colleagues in the association. Additionally, they may be called upon to represent the views of the information profession in general.

Their public relations responsibilities may include lobbying for state or national legislations and making the public aware of the significance of libraries and information centers. They may organize conferences or conventions where educational programs for members, the business of the association, exhibits of professional materials and library equipment, and entertainment all need to be coordinated effectively. These positions, like those in the various national associations of librarians and information scientists, are highly visible and influential; but the demands they make in terms of travel and general workload often mean that the individuals who accept such positions work in them for only a few years. Since there is a need for practitioners in the field to know something of the workings of their associations and for the associations' staff members to be conversant with the field's work and views, this kind of interchange is probably healthy.

Library and Information Science Faculty

Experienced librarians work in another specialty within the information professions that is usually arrived at after experience in the field. They become faculty members in a college or university program. Some teach in undergraduate education programs, preparing students to be school library media specialists, supervising them in their fieldwork in school library media centers, and teaching such courses as children's literature and basic cataloging. Other educators may have responsibility for students enrolled in two-year or one-year library technical assistant programs, where their course work may include introductory courses in librarianship. These educators may be responsible for advising students who are taking courses such as business English, typing and filing, or others that are not limited in scope to libraries but are relevant to the work for which they are preparing. These library educators may have responsibility for supervising their students on field assignments as well as placing their students, especially in their first positions.

Educators who are faculty members in graduate programs of education for the information professions often teach courses that are more theoretical than those at the undergraduate level. These are directed toward a variety of prospective information careers. In institutions where doctoral programs in library and information science are offered, educators' responsibilities include research, publishing, and close liaison with the field through their work as consultants or teachers in continuing education programs.

The full-time faculty members in any kind of information education programs usually provide most of the instruction; often their work is strengthened by that of practicing librarians who teach in their areas of expertise, perhaps on a regular part-time basis or for a summer session or workshop. Usually, the full-time faculty members must meet all requirements for faculty appointment at their institutions; doctoral degrees often are a part of this requirement. Other desirable characteristics include researching ability, teaching, competence, and general experience.

Because librarianship is a profession that requires knowledge of administration, management, and organization of information, and because it may be related to such areas as publishing, historical research, communication, and formal education, the faculty members of library education programs often have come from other areas of specialization. Social scientists, linguists, engineers, publishers, and educational administrators are among those who have served effectively on the faculties of some programs. From this, it's apparent that positions in information education are not limited to librarians. Duties in admissions and placement, editing school publications, and other varied work may not require the expertise of a faculty member. In some cases there may be others, some of them librarians, who hold these types of positions in library education programs.

Information science programs in institutions of higher education usually consist of faculty members in many different specialties. Research in information science usually is performed by faculty members in these programs, and, in this fairly new field, they are often key people in determining the nature of the field and its future.

This survey of library employment locations and types of library positions demonstrates that an extraordinary diversity of opportunities exists. Whatever your interest, special background, or education, there is likely to be an appropriate type of library work available.

Work of Support Staff

Though this book primarily addresses the career opportunities for professionally trained information professionals, we need to take note of the variety of personnel necessary to ensure the proper running of a library or information center.

In libraries, as in other places of employment, the need exists for a range of support personnel. Word processors, maintenance engineers, and security officers are only a few of the types of support staff employed. In most instances, their duties in a library may not differ much from what they might be in another work setting. For example, a guard who patrols a large academic library on a regular basis checking for fires, vandalism, or someone in trouble may really be doing the same kind of work as that of a guard in an industrial plant. Though these jobs are important to libraries, the people who perform them usually do not consider themselves as having library careers. There are, however, many people working in library support roles, and though they may not have a master's degree, they nonetheless enjoy library and information science careers. Descriptions of some of these positions follow.

Library Technician

An important member of the support staff is the library technician, sometimes designated as *library technical assistant (LTA)*. The library technician has usually completed two years of academic work, often in a community college, emphasizing the learning of library skills. Library technicians are prepared to work in public service areas as well as in technical services. Circulation routines, work on the physical preparation of books (labeling, duplicating cards, assisting with placement of orders), and such individual specialties as assisting with the maintenance and use of audiovisual equipment may be the regular work of library technicians.

Library technicians, like librarians, often are able to use the skills they have acquired elsewhere. For example, the ability to work in graphics may be applied to the preparation of instructional transparencies in a school library media center, the production of signs and exhibits for an entire public library system, or the design of an information center's annual report in a special library.

In recent years many people have attended programs that trained them for library technical assistance and have received academic credit, associate degrees, and certificates of completion. At the same time demand for library technicians has been so great that others have found exactly the kinds of positions they sought without finishing their educational programs. Their on-the-job training has enabled them to become valued members of library teams because of their particular libraries' procedures. Consequently, they often have felt no need to return to a campus to complete a training program for library technical assistants.

Some libraries have used the designation of *library technical assistant* for many members of their specialized support staff, despite the fact that they may not meet specific LTA educational requirements. Though only those trained on the job have to compete with academically trained LTAs for jobs, it may be possible that in the future, educational programs for LTAs will prove themselves so superior as a personnel source that libraries will insist on this kind of education as a prerequisite for employment. At present, however, it is more likely that libraries will continue to employ people with a mix of academic backgrounds in technical assistant positions. Because their competencies may be more related to one library than to others, those who have not completed formal training programs may find their mobility from one library to another somewhat limited.

Opportunities for members of the support staff with library experience may lead to responsible positions such as heads of circulation services, supervisors of clerical and technical personnel in some large departments, or supervisors of such support staff as equipment maintenance workers, drivers, and others. These supervisory positions customarily require unusual knowledge about the library, willingness to accept responsibility and to exercise authority, and special supervisory abilities in dealing with people. Such positions tend to be among the best available to members of the support staff, and they offer many satisfactions.

Library Assistant

Another important member of the library support staff is the library assistant. Library assistants organize library resources and make them available to users. They assist librarians and, in some cases, library technicians.

Library assistants—sometimes referred to as *library media assistants, library aides,* or *circulation assistants*—register patrons so they can borrow materials from the library. They record the borrower's name and address from an application and then issue a library card. Most library assistants enter and update patrons' records using computer databases.

At the circulation desk, assistants lend and collect books, periodicals, videotapes, and other materials. When an item is borrowed, assistants stamp the due date on the material and record the patron's identification from his or her library card. They inspect returned materials for damage, check due dates, and compute fines for overdue material. They review records to compile a list of overdue materials and send out notices. They answer patrons' questions and refer those they cannot answer to a librarian.

Throughout the library, assistants sort returned books, periodicals, and other items and return them to their designated shelves, files, or storage areas. They locate materials to be loaned, either for a patron or another library. Many card catalogs are computerized, so library assistants must be familiar with the computer system. If any materials have been damaged, these workers try to repair them. For example, they use tape or paste to repair torn pages or book covers and other specialized processes to repair the more valuable materials.

Some library assistants specialize in helping patrons who have vision problems. Sometimes referred to as *library clerks, talking-books clerks,* or *Braille-and-talking-books clerks,* they review the borrower's list of desired reading material and locate those materials or closely related substitutes from the library collection of large-type or Braille volumes, tape cassettes, and open-reel talking books. They complete the paperwork and give or mail requested materials to the borrower.

Bookmobile Driver

To extend library services to more patrons, many libraries operate bookmobiles. *Bookmobile drivers* take trucks stocked with books to designated sites on a regular schedule. Bookmobiles serve community organizations such as shopping centers, apartment complexes, schools, and nursing homes. They help extend library services to patrons living in remote areas. Depending on local conditions, drivers may operate a bookmobile alone or with a library technician.

When working alone, the drivers perform many of the same functions as a library assistant in a main or branch library. They answer patrons' questions, receive and check out books, collect fines, maintain the book collection, shelve materials, and occasionally operate audiovisual equipment to show slides or films. They participate and may assist in planning programs sponsored by the library, such as reader-advisory programs, used-book sales, or outreach programs. Bookmobile drivers keep track of their mileage, the materials lent, and the amount of fines collected. In some areas, they are responsible for maintenance of the vehicle and any photocopiers or other equipment in it. They record statistics on circulation and the number of people visiting the bookmobile. Drivers may record requests for special items from the main library and arrange for the materials to be mailed or delivered to a patron during the next scheduled visit. Many bookmobiles are equipped with personal computers and CD-ROM systems linked to the main library system; this allows bookmobile drivers to reserve or locate books immediately. Some bookmobiles offer Internet access to users.

Because bookmobile drivers may be the only link some people have to the library, much of their work is helping the public. They may assist handicapped or elderly patrons to the bookmobile or shovel snow to ensure their safety. They may enter hospitals or nursing homes to deliver books to patrons who are bedridden.

The schedules of bookmobile drivers depend on the size of the area being served. Some of these workers go out on their routes every day, while others go only on certain days. On other days, they work at the library. Some work evenings and weekends, giving patrons as much access to the library as possible.

Because such factors as personality, interest, and general competence in library-related skills are important in many support positions, these positions frequently are filled by workers who have no intention of remaining in them for any length of time but who value them either for the relevant experience or for the kind of employment opportunity they present. Members of students' families, for example, often need employment for the period of the student's enrollment at a college or university, just as the students themselves often need part-time employment. Some positions may be regularly designated for these individuals as a part of the academic institution's internal economy. Another category of people who may seek support positions on a short-term basis are those planning to enroll in library and information science education programs and who want some kind of library experience. This, of course, means that there is considerable turnover of personnel and is one reason why the position of supervisor of the support staff is an especially challenging one; staff morale and programs of in-service education become especially important in these circumstances.

The long hours that libraries usually are open require competent staff during evenings and on weekends, periods that many people want free. Because of this, work for night service supervisors, security personnel, pages, and circulation personnel may be available. These positions may appeal to students or others with daytime responsibilities. The work of re-shelving materials or preparing materials to be delivered to other library agencies may be done more efficiently at times when there are fewer users in the library, so these evening hours may be peak activity times for the staff.

Though the people who work at the libraries' charging desks are from the clerical or technical assistance ranks, they are important in establishing the climate and purpose of the library. Informal comments by these staff members about some of the library's services may stimulate users to make the most of what else is available to them. The rapport established at the circulation desk is the beginning of good interaction between the user and the library.

More service is provided to the public at a circulation desk or in a circulation department than may be visible to someone simply watching people returning or borrowing library materials. When someone has requested a specific book by title, or even by subject, for example, the circulation files are checked to determine when it is due and who has borrowed it. Some libraries provide the service of requesting its return; others promise to reserve it when it is returned. Either of these is an important service to the reader, and both require accurate records of information and careful attention to details of book circulation.

Information Society

As the world becomes more reliant on quickly relayed information for decision making, the need for individuals skilled in managing information continues to increase. From traditional professional positions in libraries to evolving positions in information centers, the opportunities for skilled personnel seem limitless. Careers range from supportive to managerial or professional, and different levels of education prepare individuals to enter this work. The next chapter outlines the types of education required for employment in the information society.

3

EDUCATION FOR THE INFORMATION PROFESSIONS

LIBRARIANS AND INFORMATION scientists come from a variety of educational backgrounds. Sometimes they designed their early schooling as a background for their future careers; later experience may have led them to change their direction to librarianship and information science. But they all discovered that professional and technical careers in librarianship and information science require carefully planned educational programs.

No significant difference exists between preparing for clerical positions in librarianship and preparing for other types of clerical positions. A high school graduation or equivalent background, knowledge of office skills and routines, and an interest in learning on the job are all important for clerical positions.

Administrators and supervisors in a library business office are referred to as *personnel officers*. Library personnel officers, as well as public relations specialists, have usually followed educational programs that prepare them for those fields. In some cases they have combined this with information education or developed expertise about libraries and information centers.

High School

Few people who later become librarians and information scientists make their career decisions before they enter college; however, subjects they take in high school do become important later. Usually their high school programs are designed to prepare them for college. In most states, the requirements for academic units in the social sciences, literature, sciences, and mathematics are sufficient if you later enter a career in library and information science. Study of one or more foreign languages may be valuable, as well. While not usually part of the precollegiate program, courses such as typing may prove valuable both for the future college student preparing papers and for the future information science professional who will work with computers online.

Extracurricular activities, which are good indicators of future interests, provide useful experience for the future. Work as a computer tutor, library assistant, or media aide during high school prepares individuals for their careers; however, you should be aware that if such work stresses only the routine aspects of library work, you may become convinced that librarianship bores you. But don't be too hasty, as it's probably a false impression. Working in a creative professional library offers the kind of challenge that is missing when you are shelving books, writing overdue slips, delivering projectors to classrooms on schedule, or performing similar mundane tasks.

Experience with responsibility and the ability to recognize the need for unglamorous behind-the-scenes work are strong assets you'll gain from working as a student assistant in a computer center library. You will have an opportunity to learn the importance of schedules on public service desks and the need for tact in dealing with library patrons. These types of information and experience are worth acquiring, but they can be gained in other ways as well: staffing concession stands at athletic games, working on the school newspaper, or accepting leadership roles in student government, for example.

High school years may be the time when young people make serious efforts to explore various careers. Many young people with no interest in information work become intrigued when they have opportunities to read about or, better yet, visit and observe other kinds of libraries or information centers. School counselors often stimulate interest, suggest visits and interviews, and locate reading materials that may be helpful.

If this kind of counseling is not available but you believe you may be interested in information-related work, you can start by interviewing librarians you know. Ask them about their own backgrounds, what satisfies them about the field, and what suggestions they would offer you. Consider them in terms of their relevance to your own career and life goals. For example, if the school librarian tells you that it was only after twenty years of teaching that she decided to enter librarianship and that it is best to start after a long period of teaching experience, you may wish to weigh that advice against your own eagerness to enter the profession for the long-term. Other people's advice only contributes to your information pool. You make the final decision.

Choosing a College

Choosing a college can be critical to your career. Certainly if you intend to study information subjects during your college years, you should plan to enter a college where this is offered regularly as part of a planned program. Often this means taking courses that are part of the education or teacher-training program. Discover if the college is accredited by a regional accrediting agency. Learn if the teacher education program is accredited by the national agency that evaluates such curricula. Direct inquiries will usually provide this information.

Many universities develop undergraduate programs in information studies. Universities that offer graduate work in library and information science often allow you to enroll in some of these courses while you are still an undergraduate.

The choice of a college is important for anyone who plans to study librarianship or information science at the graduate level. Be concerned with the quality of the college, and figure out if it is accredited by the appropriate regional accrediting agency.

Make sure that the school offers the blend of structure and flexibility you want from your college courses. Find out if it offers study abroad; it is a good way to improve your language skills. As early as possible and preferably before enrolling, make certain that the program you want is feasible. Check that the major you have in mind can be changed without penalty of lost time. It can be difficult, but try to ascertain how many of a college's graduates are admitted to their choice of graduate programs. It's important that you learn about it, both formally and informally. Make the effort to talk with students and graduates from the college about this as well as their other experiences there. In short, be sure the college provides what you want and what you might want or need before graduation.

With all these considerations in selecting a college, keep in mind that the college experience should be satisfying in itself and provide you with knowledge, experience, friends, memories, and a rich supply of opportunities. College is an investment in your future for you, your family, and the college. Choosing the right college is crucial for many reasons, not just its effect on your possible career opportunities.

The choice of a program for education as a library technical assistant usually is more restricted and often may be delayed for some years after high school graduation. Since most of these programs are in two-year community colleges, students who enroll in them usually come from the surrounding area. If you are interested, verify how frequently the various courses are offered, how many instructors there are for the courses, and what measures of success there are for the students who have completed the programs in terms of placement opportunities, advancement on the job, and other important factors.

Scarcely a subject area exists that does not relate to one of the information fields. In the information professions, a broad undergraduate preparation in the liberal arts is the best preparation for success. Certain types of library and information centers, such as agricultural libraries or toxicology research institutes, may require a specific undergraduate concentration; however, in general, any undergraduate preparation can be used in an information center.

As more and more library and information retrieval functions continue to become computer-based, all information professionals will need to be computer literate. Taking some computer courses will help you. Other undergraduate courses that might be useful include statistics, communications, business management, and research.

Selecting a Library and Information Science Program

College is the time to carefully consider the exact requirements of the library and information science education programs that you plan to enter at the graduate level. Preparing applications, gathering reference letters, planning financial arrangements for study, taking required tests, and arranging interviews or visits to the campus all usually take more time than you would expect. If you intend to start graduate school immediately or within a few months after graduation, start these tasks early in your senior year.

Before applying to schools, select three or four that appeal to you the most. Colleges should promptly answer a letter or telephone call requesting their catalog and application form. More specific questions may be directed to the schools when you go for an interview or the next time you write or call. The catalog should answer the most important questions about the school's academic program, including:

- What are the requirements for admission?
- What is the school's job placement record?
- Is financial aid available?
- What are the prospects for part-time employment?
- Who are the faculty?
- How large is the student body?

The answers to these questions may prompt others about housing near the school, access to research libraries, and availability of other financial assistance programs. Numerous scholarships and fellow-ships exist for graduate study in librarianship and information science. They are often announced in the various professional journals and compiled by such organizations as the American Library Association (ALA). In addition, service clubs, alumni groups, small foundations, church groups, or other organizations may offer financial assistance for qualifying students. Competition can be fierce for the major scholarship and fellowship programs. Don't let it deter you from trying to get such assistance. You should apply for smaller grants for which fewer people may apply or be eligible. Of course, make sure you meet the requirements of each scholarship program. Some might, for example, require the recipient to work in a public library in a particular state for a set period of time after graduating from a program of library and information science.

The answers you get to your first questions may help you decide which library and information science program you wish to attend, but it is still wise to apply to more than one for many reasons. First and foremost, you may not be accepted by your first choice; you can then move on to your second or even third choice with less effort if you have made several applications at the start of your search for a school.

It is important to choose a school where the master's degree program in library and information science is accredited by the American Library Association. The ALA accredits programs in both the United States and Canada. The standards for accreditation published by the association cover such areas as faculty, students, physical facility, administration, governance, and curriculum. Some of these may seem to indirectly affect students, but the extent to which a school is autonomous within the university or college could be important if decisions about budgeting or who shall be admitted are made without consideration of their possible contributions to the field of library and information science. Accreditation in itself does not mean that one program is superior to another that is not accredited or has not achieved accreditation for other reasons. It does mean that an outside agency has carefully reviewed the program, assessed it, and considers the program a good one. Graduation from an accredited program is important when seeking employment and might be considered an absolute requirement by many employers.

Many people may graduate from college and decide to take some time off from study and class work before continuing their education. This is quite common among those entering the information professions. A number of second-career people or reentry individuals have entered library and information careers and used their previous education and experience fruitfully.

The scope of information careers ranges from support staff to public or technical service to administration and teaching. Each level of employment requires a different category of educational preparation.

Library and Information Center Technical Assistant Programs

Community college programs are the most common for focused training of library and information center technical assistants. Positions for this type of work are not always clearly defined, but the term *library technical assistant (LTA)* is the most common one used to describe people who have completed the course work. Some libraries and information centers have included positions in their personnel structures that are designed for these individuals. More often, the library and information center technical assistants have created positions for themselves that use their skills effectively.

What are those skills? Often some postsecondary education of a general nature (English, word processing, computer programming, or accounting, for example) is needed for library and information center technical assistants. But their area of concentration probably includes courses introducing them to the information professions in general, which makes them aware of the many types of libraries, their patterns of services and purposes, and general trends. LTAs are often assigned to circulation work and technical services. Courses that teach filing routines, record-keeping, and general bibliographic control and electronic communications are a part of the curricula. Many programs include specific courses in the production of graphics, the production and utilization of other media, and an introduction to some information-seeking skills. Fieldwork or practice work in neighboring libraries is often a part of the student's academic program. This feature can be a definite asset if good performance leads to placement in the system of the library where the student has performed fieldwork.

Most programs of education for LTAs are in two-year community colleges, but they may be one- or two-year programs. The component of the program dealing with the work of library and information center technical assistants may be designed as the second year, following a more general first year of study. The programs often are closely related to the learning resources center in the community the college services. The practical emphasis of these programs, however, is such that their graduates often have much to offer in the way of skills, and they usually find no problems being placed.

The people most likely to be happy in the careers for which LTA education prepares them are those who want to work in libraries or media centers using their special skills and possibly becoming the supervisor of others who are performing technical work in those libraries. Some further specialization, perhaps in book repair, development of more skills related to electronic resources, or work on computer network systems, may be possible on the job, but advancement to professional positions in most library and information center settings is unlikely without further education

Employers typically require applicants to have at least a high school diploma or its equivalent, although many employers prefer to hire assistants with a higher level of education. Regardless of formal qualifications, most employers prefer workers who are computer literate. Knowledge of word processing and spreadsheet software is especially valuable, as is experience working in an office and good interpersonal skills.

Once hired, records processing clerks usually receive on-the-job training. Under the guidance of a supervisor or other senior worker, new employees learn company procedures and database maintenance skills. Some formal classroom training may be necessary, for instance, training in specific computer software.

College Courses in Library and Information Science

Education for information careers begun as part of undergraduate education is less common today than it was thirty or forty years ago. The demand for greater specialization, a broad liberal arts or science background, and the availability of educational programs at the graduate level in library and information science have caused many colleges that offered minors or majors in librarianship to drop their courses. In some instances, they have made drastic revisions resulting in the courses becoming graduate-level programs.

Recently, however, a number of graduate programs in library and information science have reassessed the role of undergraduate study. They have instituted information resources management programs that are intended to prepare individuals to combine another undergraduate major with a major in information studies. Since this movement is relatively new, prospective students who wish to major in the information sciences at the undergraduate level should contact an accredited program of library and information science listed in Appendix B for further information.

School Library Media Specialization at the Undergraduate Level

The need for school library media specialists, and the fact that many of their educational programs are as closely associated with schools or departments of education as they are with schools of library and information science, means that many of these media programs have been designed for those who wish to enter the school library media field. You may be working toward a major in library science or education with a minor in the other.

Emphasis

The media center courses in programs of this kind usually stress school library media center administration rather than general library management. Materials that are studied and evaluated in greatest detail are usually those designed for the clientele of school library media centers. Because of the emphasis that school library media centers usually place on instructional technology, these may be studied in greater detail than they would be in graduate programs of library and information science. Because school library media collections are relatively small, the organization of materials may be handled through a central district processing center or through specialized computer programs.

Depending on the rapport between the school library media education program and the program of teacher education at the same institution, there may be considerable emphasis on the teaching aspects of the library or media center. Instruction in how to teach library or study skills may be part of the curriculum; regardless of whether you are enrolled in the education courses, you may be encouraged or required to take one or more courses introducing you to the general field of elementary or secondary education. Since it is important for school library media specialists to know the milieu of the whole school and to have good general knowledge of the curriculum, these courses may be quite valuable.

Certification

Certification is almost universally required in school teaching positions, including library media positions. For that reason most undergraduate programs that prepare librarians for school work are carefully designated so that those completing the program will qualify for certification at least in the state where the institution is located. Two trends increase the value of that certification. One is the increase in reciprocity among states. This means that if you earn a valid certificate in one state, you may automatically be granted a certificate in another state, even though there may be slight variations in the specific requirements of the two states.

The other is the trend toward competency-based education, which is especially strong in programs of teacher education. This means that the acquisition of a specific group of competencies is recognized as necessary, and if you can demonstrate possession of those competencies, you have met the requirements. In programs like this, the accumulation of academic credit is valueless unless you have acquired the competencies judged necessary for the work.

School library media education programs at the undergraduate level customarily require practice or fieldwork in a school library media center. This may be taken in conjunction with practice teaching; both may be required at different times, or the library media fieldwork may be sufficient. Because school library media specialists are likely to be employed, at least in their first jobs, in settings where they must work independently and with limited or no access to a supervisor with background in librarianship, it is especially important for them to experience working with a certified media specialist.

There was a time when school library media specialists came exclusively from the ranks of experienced classroom teachers. As recognition of the special background and work of librarians has increased, there have been increasing numbers who entered the field directly. It is still customary for them to have certification as teachers and to have demonstrated, at least through practice teaching, their ability to teach. For that reason, a typical program of courses for a college student intending to become a school library media specialist includes such general courses as English, history, or science along with professional education courses such as teaching reading and social studies, history of American or western education, curriculum, and educational psychology. The component of library and media science education typically includes children's literature, school media library administration, media selection, cataloging and classification, reference, and instructional technology.

Computer Literacy

Many state certifying agencies include computer literacy as a requirement for school library media positions for two reasons:

- Computer laboratories often are located in or adjacent to school library media centers. Since these are a schoolwide resource, they are viewed by school administrators as analogous to the media center in their centrality to the educational enterprise.
- Many computer software programs enable school library media librarians to automate their own circulation, acquisitions, and cataloging operations.

As the typical program suggests, this curriculum can be a demanding one, especially since it may include one or more assignments for practice or fieldwork in schools. The graduate of such a program may be disappointed to discover that some top jobs in the field of school media librarianship, such as district supervisors, are reserved for those who have completed advanced degrees in library and information science. In fact, most school systems place so much emphasis on the need for continuing education that they encourage librarians to take courses by paying higher salaries to those with advanced degrees or by reimbursing students wholly or partially for their tuition expenses. Many school media specialists who leave their colleges thinking they will take a rest from education find that before long they are taking more courses, either on a part-time basis or during summer school.

Graduates of undergraduate library education programs may decide to pursue other areas of interest in their advanced academic work. Because of the heavy emphasis on professional education courses during their college years, this may be a wise decision. One possibility is entering a master's degree program in library and information science with the intention of changing to another specialization within the field. As former school media librarians prepare for another phase in their careers, they may take a broad range of courses relating, for example, to special libraries and their media or to the particular problems of public libraries.

Undergraduate programs of this kind are probably best if you want to begin working immediately after college and you are sure that school media librarianship appeals to you. It's important to recognize that later shifts in career goals may present problems. However, this career has many satisfactions. If you are interested in school library media centers, it's important to recognize that many states are moving toward certification requiring a master's degree, so you should contact the department of education in the states where you are interested in working to determine the latest qualifications needed.

Library and Information Center Associate Positions

Many libraries have positions designated for library associates, those individuals who have completed four years of college but who may have little or no academic preparation in library or information science. Although positions of this kind may not be satisfying enough for a life's career, they may be attractive to those intending to prepare themselves for librarianship or another career by further study or to those who wish to work in libraries for a few years. Typical of the positions and responsibilities assigned to library associates may be assistance in some of the library's technical services, such as online searching for cataloging information; outreach work in public libraries, often with special emphasis on work with children; providing telephone reference service; and assisting with promotional activities of the library, such as editing a newsletter or designing exhibits and graphic materials.

It is rare to find college curricula designed to prepare library associates for their work. Almost any academic background can be helpful to the library associate, from art to zoology. The reliance that libraries place on library associates has caused some people to discuss the possibility of more precisely designed academic programs in this area. Included in these programs would be undergraduate courses that act as good introductions to satisfying careers in librarianship. If these develop to any extent in the next few years, they may be useful and available for would-be library associates. In the meantime, the position of library associate is one that may be sought and filled by college graduates who enjoy working in a library and who want to work where they can use the education, interests, and special skills or knowledge they have acquired.

Master's Degree for the Information Professions

Preparation for the information professions at the professional level almost always requires the minimum of a master's degree. The degree may have many names—master of science, master of arts, master of information science, master of library and information science, master of library and information studies—but it denotes the completion of a planned program of study beyond the bachelor's degree, with emphasis on learning not only the skills needed for the information professions but the philosophy of the professions.

Nearly all librarians attain the master's degree from institutions that provide a major course of study in library and information science. Other aspects of information careers may substitute a master's degree in management information systems through a business administration program or a master's degree in computer science, but today most of these allied fields' subject matter is covered in programs leading to the master's degree in library and information science.

A number of library and information science programs offer joint degrees with departments of computer science, business administration, history (for archival work), law, or other disciplines. These specialties are outlined in the catalogs and bulletins of the programs that offer them.

The master's degree in library and information science typically offers opportunities for both the pursuit of general interests and some degree of specialization that parallels opportunities for professional work. Most students begin with required courses that may include an introduction to information in modern society, basic organizational skills (both manual and computerized), and management concepts. Specialization then occurs through close work with a graduate advisor in such areas as online information retrieval, academic librarianship, records management, public librarianship, systems analysis, youth services, indexing and abstracting, school library media, computer applications, health sciences information, or database management.

The course of study generally lasts from one to two years, depending on the program. Variations by university can only be identified through reading catalogs and application information that refers directly to the accredited master's degree programs listed in Appendix B.

Admissions Process

Typical requirements include a written application, perhaps an interview, evidence of foreign language skills, scores on a national examination such as the Graduate Record Examination (GRE) or on one designed by the individual school or university, and letters of reference from people who know the applicant.

The school's catalog usually details admission requirements. You should read it and other material from the school carefully, making sure that you understand what is expected of you and what you may expect from the school. Usually, the full range of courses may be listed in the catalog, but some may be limited to students in the doctoral program, if there is one. Others may be offered only occasionally. If you wish to register for some specific courses, indicate that in your correspondence or when you visit the school and verify whether those courses will be offered while you are a student. Slight or major changes in the program may occur while you are enrolled, and you should inquire in advance about how a change of requirements will affect you and, if so, in what ways.

The process of admission usually contains several steps. If you do not hear from the school within a reasonable time, check with the school's admissions officer. A letter of reference may be missing, for instance, and it may be possible to replace it. It's your responsibility to make sure the application is complete.

Courses of Study

Library and information science education programs vary considerably in the extent to which you are encouraged or permitted to register for courses in other parts of the college or university. In some programs a minor in another field is required; but in most you probably will take all or nearly all of the courses in the library and information science program. Joint programs with other schools or departments are available in some universities. Among these are ones that prepare for law librarianship by offering a program of law courses and library and information science courses, along with similar ones in business administration, education, computer science, and such area studies as Latin America, the Far East, or Southeast Asia. Especially in joint programs of this kind, you are usually at an advantage if you declare your interest in such programs at the time you apply and if you work closely with an adviser in choosing courses. This way you fill all necessary requirements as expeditiously as possible.

As in other graduate programs, those in library schools are designed for adults; therefore, emphasis on the importance of an adviser may seem strange; but it is valuable for you to become acquainted with at least one faculty member, preferably one who shares many of the same professional interests and, ideally, one with whom you are personally compatible. For example, the adviser who is aware of your interests and intentions may represent those interests to the faculty when schedule changes are being considered, especially if those changes would be to your disadvantage. In a large school, you may benefit from bonding with at least one member of the faculty, with whom you may have to take the initiative to maintain communication. Usually you register with your adviser for each term. One more conversation or brief visit each term may be sufficient.

Graduation Requirements

You should review requirements for graduation from the master's degree program. The total number of courses, the core or required courses, the grade average you must maintain, your preparation of a thesis or research project, and the passing of a comprehensive examination are all considerations among these requirements. If you want to design a highly individualized study program, avoid a school where most of the courses are specified as required and there are few elective choices.

Even if the school's requirements are fairly flexible, you must exercise judgment in designing a program for yourself. You may be tempted to select a variety of courses on the theory that you will be prepared for any kind of information work. An employer who looks at an array of courses taken by a graduate—one course in each of three types of library administration or courses that range from data structures to government documents with no set evidence of purpose or goal—is simply puzzled about the individual's interest and goals rather than impressed by a broad spectrum of skills. Management, bibliographic organization, library materials, and issues for the information society are usually represented in core or basic courses. The value of taking at least one course in each of these areas fairly early in the program is that it may help you decide what you will choose next. Systems analysis, for example, will probably have a prerequisite of introductory computer programming. If you discover you enjoy that kind of study, you may miss the opportunity to study it further if you have postponed taking introductory programming until late in your graduate program. Many choices probably will be available, even in a fairly structured program.

Earlier in this section under the heading "Selecting a Library and Information Science Program," comments were made about the value of selecting programs that are accredited by the American Library Association. During graduate study it may be worthwhile to review the reasons for selecting the program you are in. Explore ways to benefit from that selection in terms of placement, communications with others in the field who know the school, and the value of keeping in touch with the school after you complete your education.

In addition to the courses you take, you often have access to other information and experience through a school's program of colloquium talks; attendance at local, state, or national conferences of library and information associations; and field trips to libraries and information centers. The content of programs may open up new areas of interest or illuminate problems that you previously discovered. But even if that is not the case, the experience of meeting people already in the field and of sitting in on discussions of their interests and activities can be a valuable part of becoming a professional.

Education Beyond the Master's Degree

You may decide to continue your professional education beyond the master's degree for many reasons. You may wish to change from one specialization within the field to another. You may need to continue taking courses to receive salary increases or other benefits. You may want to conduct research you consider valuable to the field. You may simply want the intellectual challenge.

It is always worthwhile to ask whether further formal study is really the best means of attaining what you want and whether your goals are realistic. A rigorous program of reading, observing the work of others, and attending conferences or in-service meetings prepares you to enter a new specialization within the field. This type of program may be much more economical in time and energy than enrolling in formal courses.

You may decide to acquire advanced degrees elsewhere before entering the information professions. Many people seek further study in other areas. Sometimes they want to improve proficiency as a librarian. For example, an art librarian works toward a degree in art history, or another librarian who began working in personnel decides to become more expert in that field. Sometimes the further study may be simply for pleasure or personal satisfaction. Other times someone wants to change to another career.

The fields of librarianship and information science offer many programs for post-master's degree study that differ in purpose and content. Study for a certificate of advanced study, a doctoral degree, and for general continuing education may be appropriate at different points in your career. Naturally you would need comprehensive information about their relative values, scope, and purpose.

Certificates of Advanced Study

As interest in continuing professional education has increased, many individuals have also shown interest in working toward specific goals. In many schools of library and information science, programs of study that award certificates for program completion have been introduced. Sometimes they are referred to as "specialist's certificates," "certificates of advanced study," or "sixth-year certificates," the last term indicating that they are awarded for completion of a sixth year of study beyond high school. Customary requirements include the completion of a group of courses, usually selected in advance from those available in the school of library and information science or elsewhere in the university. A research paper may be required, although research is not a major component of this program. The certificate can usually be attained in one academic year of full-time study or by part-time study over a longer period of time.

Certificate programs are not the same as degree programs. Those who question the awarding of a certificate should keep in mind that it provides recognition for the completion of a set program, not simply for the acquisition of a number of academic credits. The program may be especially good if you are considering enrolling in a doctoral program but are not sure your interest and competence are great enough to overcome the obstacles of returning to academic study after working a few years. However, the entire thrust of these programs is usually quite different from those of doctoral programs. As noted, certificate programs designed for practitioners in the information field are usually short-range in time and chiefly consist of course work. Success in the courses determines whether you will receive the certificate.

Doctoral Programs

Almost every one of the characteristics delineated for certificate programs is the opposite for doctoral study. Doctoral programs are typically more structured, with a series of examinations and set requirements designed by the school that offers them. At one time, doctoral programs were chiefly designed for those who wished to devote their careers to teaching and research. However, the demand for more skills in the field of administration—especially in research, academic, and school libraries—has led to the development of doctoral programs in which research plays a less significant role. The Ph.D., or doctor of philosophy degree, usually indicates research emphasis, while the D.L.S., or doctor of library science degree, is usually classified as a professional degree rather than a research degree. These distinctions are not clear-cut. Some institutions offer one degree, but the requirements are similar to a degree elsewhere with a different title. The Doctor of Arts, the newest doctoral degree in librarianship, is usually carefully specified for practitioners only, with no research component.

Admission to a doctoral program is usually achieved in a series of steps. You must meet requirements for admission to the school itself. Because the program's emphasis is likely to be on research, you should have some idea of the desired area of research, as well as knowledge of the faculty members and other facilities needed for conducting that research.

Courses taken by a doctoral student may be the same as those taken in master's degree programs, especially if some years have elapsed since the doctoral student received the master's degree. Some schools, incidentally, require that students entering the doctoral program must have worked a certain number of years. In any case it is the examinations and research that are important for success in the doctoral program, rather than success in course work. Proof of proficiency in one or more foreign languages may be required at this stage of a student's program.

The identification of a topic for doctoral research is customarily based on extensive reading, sometimes on preliminary research or a feasibility study, and on the interests and abilities of the potential researcher. Usually you must develop a proposal stating what you intend to do in the research and present evidence of the value of the research. A faculty committee probably will review and evaluate the work at that time, perhaps by conducting an oral examination to determine the value of the topic and the student's ability to conduct the research. From that point on in a doctoral program, you may work almost entirely independently, collecting data for the study, analyzing the data, perhaps traveling to interview individuals who have information or insights, and finally writing a dissertation based on the findings. You must defend this work, usually orally, to a faculty group.

A faculty committee may be responsible for the doctoral program. It decides on admissions and designs the general examinations. That committee may then designate yet another committee, consisting of the student's adviser and two or three other members to serve as the student's committee. The defense of the dissertation may be made before the entire faculty, the student's committee, or the doctoral committee. In some recent variations, you present this defense before your peers—fellow students or other interested people in the university community—as well. This defense is usually the final step in getting a doctoral degree.

While some schools consider three years as the customary length of time for students seeking doctoral degrees, longer periods are not uncommon. The usual difficulty comes in selecting a topic and organizing the findings and data of research. It is at these times that many doctoral candidates withdraw, either formally or informally, from the program. This can be traumatic, not only for the individual but for his or her family, adviser, friends, and colleagues. For this reason it is important that if you are considering a doctoral program, carefully assess the resources—intellectual, physical, and financial—required for the prolonged effort you may need to make.

The kinds of research conducted in the library and information fields at the doctoral level vary considerably. The following dissertation titles provide an idea of the range of topics and methods:

- "A Role Transformed? Technology's Challenge for Job Responsibilities of the Reference Librarian"
- "A Qualitative Study of How Librarians at a Public Research University Envision Their Work and Work Lives"
- "The Role of the High School Library Media Program in Three Nationally Recognized South Carolina Blue Ribbon Secondary Schools"
- "The Changing Print Resource Base of Academic Libraries in the United States: A Comparison of Collection Patterns in Seventy-Two ARL Academic Libraries of Nonserial Imprints for the Years 1995 and 2000"

Research acts as a main link between those who work in the information professions and those engaged in library and information science education. Many investigations of feasibility of innovation techniques have come from research centers in educational programs. The experience of identifying a problem, solving or attempting to solve it, and reporting on the process is often valuable for someone who later becomes a practitioner and must deal with problems in the same way. The objective view of the experienced researcher is important when task forces or other action groups are planning new or revised library programs.

Continuing Education

Information science and librarianship have numerous programs in continuing education, in addition to the more formally constructed programs for doctoral study or certificates of advanced study. The typical purposes of continuing education include the introduction of new techniques, such as computer-assisted reference service, or the continued development of special skills, such as storytelling. Some programs are repeated regularly, as is the case with several university-sponsored programs in library administration and management. Universities, professional and educational associations, and government agencies act as the most frequent sponsors of continuing education programs.

Institute, seminar, conference, workshop—these are only four of the designations used for the variety of programs available, and they are often used with no clear distinction among them.

Less readily identified as continuing education programs are the many offerings of library systems, corporations, or educational institutions in which librarians and information specialists are employed. These may include orientation programs for new employees, regularly scheduled meetings for selection of media, programs on new techniques or services, or much more general activities, such as lectures or media presentations introducing personnel to the community or to cultural events. Employers that provide these programs probably have a commitment to continuing education. As a prospective employee, you would benefit from inquiring about such opportunities, as well as about the extent to which the institution may support attendance at other continuing education events.

Somewhat different from the continuing education programs are conferences sponsored by associations representing the library and information science professions. Most of these groups sponsor annual conferences at which exhibits of equipment and media, formal meetings, less formal workshops, the business and committee work of the association, social events, placement interviews, and much professional conversation and communication are major events.

Your best plan for continuing education is the one that supplies an opportunity to increase your skills or expertise on your present job, offers some satisfaction in the accomplishment of an educational program, and possibly prepares you for another position or a different specialization.

Many options abound, although your own finances or those of your employer may create limitations. Nonetheless, you should be able to create a career path for yourself that proves satisfying and that provides opportunities for you to use and more fully develop your abilities.

4

PLACEMENT OF
INFORMATION PROFESSIONALS

PLACEMENT PATTERNS AND practices for nonprofessional and professional positions in library and information services differ. For nonprofessional positions, prospective employers and employees often are only concerned with local applicants. However, professional positions are more likely to be announced in national publications, and recruits are sought from a broader geographic area.

Because of this, personnel placement in clerical and technical positions is much like placement in other fields. You may find openings in classified advertisements in newspapers or through a telephone call to a school system or public library. If you know someone in a position at a good company, ask him or her to give a word-of-mouth referral to the employer. Such referrals often result in jobs.

Professional placement, usually handled quite differently and for a fee, is much more complicated; but this, too, may result in a satisfying position.

Initial Placement

Most people see the first professional position after graduation as significant because it provides valuable experience. It also gives you an opportunity to test yourself and your previous education as you learn more about the profession you are entering. Finding and getting this kind of position is worth the energy and thought required to find it.

A portion of your senior year in college may be occupied with assembling the information and resources you need to apply to a library education program. Similarly, you will probably devote a portion of your professional education to planning your initial placement. Randomly reading lists of positions as they appear in the publications mentioned in the Suggested Reading is a beginning. But the time comes when you, the potential applicant, need to study those positions more carefully and relate the job requirements to your own competencies. Consider whether the work described, the geographic area, or the kind of library is most appropriate for you. You may need to make some mental adjustments and determine if ideas about salary are realistic in terms of the available positions.

You probably will find assistance on your own campus at various stages of this process. Faculty members may be willing to advise you about the range of opportunities or recommend you for, or inform you about, specific positions. Since their general responsibilities are to all the students, not just to one, their interest and time may be limited. Most schools post announcements of openings, provide copies of journals and papers that include advertisements for positions, and offer seminars or discussions by administrators who are responsible for personnel. Placement counselors may inform you about the task of finding and getting a position.

Early Opportunities

Some of the most satisfying initial placements occur when students find positions in settings where they are already working. Many libraries and information centers employ students. Although student employment does not guarantee you a future position, the alert student who has performed effectively has one foot in the door when a beginning professional position opens. Keep this in mind when you seek a part-time position while enrolled in school.

Another kind of opportunity may be available to those who successfully compete for the various available internships or work-study programs. Typically, these also stipulate that the intern should not expect the experience to lead to a job offer, but in reality this is a possibility. In addition, some other research libraries, academic libraries, and other kinds of libraries may offer internship programs. The bases on which these are run may vary considerably in terms of formality, their link with library education programs, and the opportunity they offer. Because potential employers consider prior experience to be important, the fact that you have acquired such experience is often valuable in itself.

Sources of Help

Although there are helpful resources for you when seeking your first professional position, it is your responsibility to take the initiative and follow through. The suggestions must be yours. Others may inform, advise, and recommend, but you must decide what you will apply for, if you can invest in travel for interviews, and if there are some areas of the country, or some kinds of library positions, that you will not consider—in short, the investment you are willing to make in your search for a position.

What are some of these resources? How can you find and use them to your advantage? The Internet provides a variety of valuable resources for job seekers in the library profession. An excellent source of information about Internet resources is the 2008–2009 *Guide to Internet Job Searching* by Margaret Riley Dikel and Frances Roehm, published by the Public Library Association and McGraw-Hill. This guide includes a section specifically for library and information sciences that lists websites, Listservs, and bulletin boards. One website is www.rileyguide.com.

Another excellent source of library employment resources on the Internet is the Internet Public Library, a worldwide website maintained at the University of Michigan with links to academic and professional association listings, searchable databases, compiled guides, mailing lists, and some nonlibrary-specific Internet sites. To access the Internet Public Library, connect to www.ipl.org and search for the "Library Employment" page via the link "Especially for Librarians." Another site, www.lisjobs.com, offers library job listings provided by Library Job Postings on the Internet and www.lisjobs.com. These are jointly maintained by Sarah Johnson and Rachel Singer Gordon.

You should also contact the university's or the library school's placement service. Learn the terms on which it is available, such as whether a fee is charged and whether service is limited to graduates. If you believe its services are useful, you should use them but without relying exclusively on them. Some placement services provide information about jobs, others handle credentials and submit them to prospective employers, and many perform both of these services. Handling credentials is a time-consuming task and can help the student. In this way, letters of reference can be collected at one time and sent out on request, so you do not have to solicit them repeatedly.

For some positions, usually those in academic libraries or school libraries and also for entrance to another academic program, you may need your library school transcripts. These usually are handled by the registrar's office for a fee, but it is a good idea to find out how to get them quickly and efficiently as you may have to provide them with little notice. Official transcripts usually must be sent to a third party, another educational institution, or a prospective employer; they are not sent directly to the student or graduate.

Although the university's placement service may be the most important single channel for information and assistance in seeking a position, it may be supplemented with more informal channels. Faculty members, fellow students, bulletin board or other kinds of announcements, and librarians or information scientists among the school's alumni also may provide information.

Some of the various agencies available to assist in placement in general are listed later in this chapter. Information of this kind may become rapidly outdated as the placement scene changes in various parts of the country and as informal means of communication increase. Local library and information science associations may provide assistance in placement, perhaps by posting positions at meetings or by maintaining a file of positions available.

Individuals in the profession in key positions are likely to hear about opportunities. They may be placement officers in libraries, staff members of professional associations, or library and information science education faculty members. If they are aware of your needs and interests, they may be able to help you find the kind of position you want. Those who may have encouraged you to enter the profession may be able to provide personal assistance and information. Like the other groups and individuals who may assist, these people are better able to do so if you provide them with accurate, current information about yourself. For instance, providing them with résumés that have been carefully prepared for employers and letting them know what your present status and hopes are can be important moves on your part.

Midcareer Placement

Librarians and information scientists are, on the whole, a fairly mobile group of people. Among the most mobile are those with an eagerness to work in different kinds of settings, a strong sense of purpose, and a willingness to take some risks. Even those who stay in one library system may consider their options for other kinds of placement from time to time and may have to use some of the same techniques as they would use if they were changing systems.

Occasionally, advancement or change occurs spontaneously: your supervisor retires or resigns and you are promoted to the position; or work on the committee of a professional association brings you into contact with the director of another library, who urges you to accept a position there. You may help develop a new service and then become the person responsible for it.

Mental Alarm Clock

Ideally, you need a kind of mental alarm clock to keep track of how long you have been doing the same thing, whether there is still challenge in a job, and what kind of move you should make next to achieve your goal. It is usually only in fiction that the unknown person at the fourth desk back is invited to become head of the corporation. In real life, before an employee is chosen to accept a major administrative assignment, experience needs to be acquired, often in a variety of settings or in a variety of specializations, and usually with increasing responsibility.

The mental alarm clock also should remind you of the need for current letters of reference, which may be added to your original placement file and which may be much easier to acquire at times when you are not actively seeking a position. Supervisors might write these after an evaluation interview, or colleagues might be asked to write them after completion of some major project.

Some people like to keep their placement files active at all times, so they can be informed of potential positions they may want to consider. Others do so only when they are actively seeking a change. In a more casual way, nearly everyone tracks the announcements of available positions to compare their experience, academic background, and salary with the criteria and benefits offered for these other positions. Even a quick review of the announcements of new appointments to positions can keep you informed of classmates, former colleagues, or other acquaintances. Keep aware of their changes of position as they may interest you if your current position has begun to lose its challenge.

There is certainly more likelihood that you will be sought out for a job in the middle of your career than there is when you are initially employed. The general quality of your work, written reports, or activity in professional associations may call you to the attention of others. So you may have to decide whether to follow up on an invitation or a suggestion that might be appealing but that has not been anticipated.

Other Reasons for Midcareer Change

Advancement is not the only reason for midcareer changes. A parent's illness, a broken marriage, a desire for travel, or a spouse's new position in another part of the country can occasionally necessitate change. In most cases like these, you will have to repeat many of the same steps followed when you sought your first position: preparing a résumé, reviewing announcements of positions, reactivating a file in the placement service, and letting friends and associates know of your plan to move. If no position equivalent in salary and responsibility with your previous position is available, you may have to consider accepting one at a lower level or perhaps make a major shift to another kind of library or to somewhat different work. Some prospective employers may be reluctant to employ you if they consider you overqualified for the available position; they may think you will be dissatisfied or bored in a position that does not provide enough challenge.

One consideration in contemplating a midcareer change is that it is at least twice as easy to get a job when you already have a job as it is to get one while unemployed. For that reason it may be a good idea to take a leave of absence rather than resign in order to enjoy a year's travel. A trip to the part of the country where you plan to move can be a reasonable investment if it means you could seek a position and schedule interviews there while still employed elsewhere.

In recent years pressures from government agencies and civil rights groups have resulted in many positions being advertised much more widely than before, but it still is possible to miss seeing announcements of appealing positions. If you are considering a midcareer change for reasons other than those relating directly to your job, make some discreet inquiries to several libraries and information centers in the prospective area. This may stimulate them to send information about openings there.

It is somewhat more difficult when problems with co-workers make a position untenable or when conscience drives you to resign. At these times, the hardest thing to do may be the most necessary:

to review the entire situation as objectively as possible, consider as many options for actions as exist, and act on them in a rational, unhurried way. Also keep in mind that in terms of future employment possibilities, an employer will often accept the fact that one situation was untenable and required a drastic move. He or she is likely, however, to look askance at a career record that involves many short-term appointments and where, according to the applicant, the problem often was the personality of others or the unreasonable demands that were made.

Length of Time on a Job

To raise the question about when to change jobs in a different way, how long should you be expected to stay on a job? For professional positions the answer would be not less than one year and, more likely, at least two years. In jobs with special responsibilities or set terms of appointment, periods of three or five years may be expected. It is important for you and your supervisor to agree on the appropriate length of time, at least in a general way. The interview may be a good time for you to raise a question about the length of time expected for the position.

But you both need to realize that the timing of a resignation is also important. If you leave at the same time someone else in the same department resigns, it can increase the impact of a resignation. Resigning just as a superior is recuperating from surgery can be almost traumatic. When you resign, observe the same consideration and courtesies that you do when you get a position: written notice, adequate time to plan for the change, and a willingness to make the transition as painless as possible.

Midcareer placement offers special challenges and concerns but is basically similar to initial placement. It may be avidly sought or thrust upon the individual, and its timing is often unpredictable. Even if you are satisfied and happy with your career, you may consider midcareer change just the same as someone who feels dissatisfied with previous positions: you need to be aware of personal strengths, weaknesses, present value to a prospective employer, future goals, and the means of attaining those goals.

Agencies Engaged in Placement Activities

In addition to the Internet-based employment sources mentioned earlier, the library placement services that follow are excerpted from the guide prepared for the *Bowker Annual Library and Book Trade Almanac* entitled *Guide to Employment Sources in the Library and Information Professions*.* It is compiled by Maxine Moore, Office for Human Resource Development and Recruitment, American Library Association.

Library Literature

Classified ads of library vacancies and positions wanted are carried in many of the national, regional, and state library journals and newsletters. Members of associations can sometimes list position-wanted ads free of charge in their membership publications. Listings of positions available are regularly found in *American Libraries*, *Chronicle of Higher Education*, *College and Research Libraries News*, *Library Journal*, www.libraryjournal.com, and *Library Hotline*. State and regional library association newsletters, state library journals,

---

*   Edited and used by permission of the Office for Library Personnel Resources of the American Library Association, updated 2006. For annual updates, see editions of the *Bowker Annual Library and Book Trade Almanac*.

foreign library periodicals, and other types of periodicals carrying such ads are listed in later sections.

Newspapers

The *New York Times* Sunday "Week in Review" section carries a special section of ads for librarian jobs in addition to the regular classifieds. Local newspapers, particularly the larger city Sunday editions, such as the *Washington Post, Los Angeles Times,* and *Chicago Tribune,* often carry job vacancy listings in libraries for both professionals and paraprofessionals. There are many Web-based versions of the newspapers and journals.

Internet

The many library-related electronic Listservs on the Internet often post library job vacancies interspersed with other news and discussion items. A growing number of general online job-search Internet sites exist, including www.career.com, www.monster.com, and www.hotjobs.com. These include information-related job notices and other types of jobs. This book includes information on electronic access where available through the individual organizations listed here. Some Internet-related resources include the following:

- "Information Professional's Guide to Career Development Online," by Sarah L. Nesbeitt and Rachel Singer Gordon, Information Today, 2002; see the companion website, www.listjobs.com/careerdev.
- "Making Short Work of the Job Search," by Marilyn Rosenthal, *Library Journal,* September 1, 1997; this includes an updated reference list.

Some library-related job-search Web links include these:

- Job listings at www.lisjobs.com
- *Ann's Place* for library positions around the world at geocities.com/aer_mcr/libjob
- Job listings in the Texas Library Association New Members Round Table at www.txla.org/groups/NMRT/index.htm.
- Online sources for what libraries own and what services they offer at www.worldcat.org
- The New York public library system at www.nypl.org/links/index.cfm
- Jobs in Florida that do not require an ALA certification at Floridalibraryjobs.org
- Job listings at http://web.syr.edu/~jryan/infopro/jobplib.html
- Library job postings at www.librarysupportstaff.com/libjobs.html
- The *Networked Librarian* at http://pw1.netcom.com/~feridun/libjobs.htm and the "Job Search Guide" at pw2.netcom.com/~feridun/nlintro.htm
- Job postings listed at *Library Juice* at libr.org/juice/issues/vol3/LJ_3.11.sup.html
- Career and job information at www.itcompany.com/inforetriever/job.htm
- Job opportunities at www.libraryjobpostings.org
- *Job Opportunities for Librarians and Library Science Net Links* at librarians.miningco.com/msubjobs.htm
- *Library Job Postings on the Internet*, compiled by Sarah Johnson at www.libraryjobpostings.org
- Asian/Pacific American Librarians Association job listings at www.apalaweb.org/jobs/apalajobs.htm. Its quarterly

newsletter also includes some job ads, and it is free to members of the Asian/Pacific American Librarians Association.

- *Chinese-American Librarians Association Newsletter* at www.cala-web.org. Job listings in its newsletter are issued in February, June, and October and is free to members.

Specialized Library Associations and Groups

A comprehensive resource on employment, voluntary service, and career development can be found at www.communityjobs.org. Also, consider the following:

Advanced Information Management
444 Castro Street, Suite 320
Mountain View, CA 94041
www.aimusa.com

and

900 Wilshire Boulevard, Suite 1424
Los Angeles, CA 90017

This placement agency specializes in library and information personnel. It offers work on a temporary, permanent, and contract basis for both professional librarians and paraprofessionals in the special, public, and academic library marketplace. It also supplies consultants who can work with special projects in libraries or manage library development projects. There is no fee to applicants.

American Association of Law Libraries Career Hotline
53 West Jackson Boulevard, Suite 940
Chicago, IL 60604
www.aallnet.org

Classified job listings are available at www.aallnet.org, grouped by type.

American Library Association
Association of College and Research Libraries
50 East Huron Street
Chicago, IL 60611
www.ala.org/acrl/c&rlnew2.html

Classified advertising appears each month in *College and Research Libraries News*. Ads appearing in the print edition are also posted to *C&RL NewsNet*, an abridged electronic edition of that publication.

American Library Association
Office for Human Resource Development and Recruitment
50 East Huron Street
Chicago, IL 60611
www.ala.org/hrdr/placemt.html

A placement service is provided at each annual conference (June or July) and midwinter meeting (January or February). Request job seeker or employer registration forms prior to each conference, or register with the service and purchase job and job-seeker listings directly from the conference site. Information is included when requesting registration forms. Handouts on interviewing, preparing a résumé, and other job-seeker information are available.

In addition to the ALA conference placement center, ALA division national conferences usually include a placement service. See the *American Libraries* "Datebook" for dates of upcoming divisional conferences. The ALA provides website job postings from *American Libraries*, *College and Research Libraries News*, the LITA Job Site, and its conference placement services through its website, www.ala.org, on the library education and employment menu page.

American Society for Information Science
8720 Georgia Avenue, #501
Silver Spring, MD 20910
www.asis.org

An active placement service is operated at American Society for
Information Science (ASIS) annual meetings (usually October,
locales change). All conference attendees—both ASIS members and
nonmembers—as well as ASIS members who cannot attend the
conference, are eligible to use the service to list or find jobs. Job
listings also are accepted from employers who cannot attend the
conference. Interviews are arranged. Throughout the year, current
job openings are listed in *ASIS Jobline*, a monthly publication sent
to all members and available to nonmembers on request with a self-
addressed, stamped envelope.

Art Libraries Society of North America
232-239 March Road, Box 11
Ottawa, ON K2K 2E1
Canada
www.arlisna.org

Art information and visual resources curator jobs are listed in the
ARLIS/NA Update six times a year, and a job registry is maintained
at the society's headquarters. Any employer may list a job with the
registry, but only members of ARLIS may request job information.
Job listings are also made available on the ARLIS-L Listserv and
website.

Association for Educational Communications and Technology
1800 North Stonelake Drive, Suite 2
Bloomington, IN 47404
www.aect.org

The Association for Educational Communications and Technology maintains a placement listing on its website and provides a placement service at the annual convention that is free to all registrants.

Association for Library and Information Science Education
65 East Wacker Place, Suite 1900
Chicago, IL 60601
www.alise.org

The Association for Library and Information Science Education provides placement services at its annual conference (January or February) for library and information studies faculty and administrative positions.

Association of Research Libraries
21 Dupont Circle NW, Suite 800
Washington, DC 20036
www.arl.org

This website lists job openings at Association of Research Libraries member libraries.

C. Berger Group
327 East Gundersen Drive
Carol Stream, IL 60188
www.cberger.com

C. Berger Group conducts executive searches to fill permanent management, supervisory, and director positions in libraries, information centers, and other organizations nationwide. Direct hire and temp-to-hire services also are available. Other employment services include supplying professional and support staff–level temporary workers and contract personnel for short- and long-term assignments in special, academic, and public libraries in Illinois, Indiana, Georgia, Texas, Wisconsin, and other states. It also provides library and information management consulting services, as well as direction and staff to manage projects for clients both on-site and off-site.

Canadian Library Association
328 Frank Street
Ottawa, ON K2P 0X8
Canada
www.cla.ca

Publishes career ads in *Feliciter* magazine, provides career ads online, and operates a job mart at its annual conference in June.

Carney, Sandoe, and Associates
136 Boylston Street
Boston, MA 02116
www.carneysandoe.com

An educational recruitment firm that places teachers and administrators in private, independent schools across the United States and overseas. It has placed more than seven thousand teachers and administrators in independent schools since 1977, and it has thousands of positions available in all primary and secondary subjects each year. All fees are paid by the hiring schools, services are free to the candidate, and teacher certification is not necessary.

Catholic Library Association
100 North Street, Suite 224
Pittsfield, MA 01201
www.cathla.org

Personal and institutional members of the Catholic Library Association are given free space (thirty-five words) to advertise for jobs or to list job openings in *Catholic Library World*, published four times per year. Nonmembers may also advertise. Contact advertising coordinator for rates.

Council on Library/Media Technicians
P.O. Box 52057
Riverside, CA 92517
http://colt.ucr.edu/ncccjob

Gossage Sager Associates/Bradbury Associates
4545 Wornall, Suite 805
Kansas City, MO 64111
www.gossagesager.com

This is an executive search firm specializing in the recruitment of library directors and other information-handling organizations' top management. Nationwide searches have been conducted since 1983 for public, academic, and specialized libraries in all U.S. regions.

Labat-Anderson
8000 Westpark Drive, Suite 400
McLean, VA 22102
www.labat.com

This is a worldwide consulting firm specializing in information systems and services, environmental services, and litigation support. It is one of the largest providers of library and records management services to the federal government. An employment link may be found on its website.

The Library Co-Op
P.O. Box 7197
Colonia, NJ 07067
www.thelibraryco-op.com/contact.htm

The Library Co-Op is licensed as both a temporary and a permanent employment agency and provides consultants for a wide variety of information settings and functions from library moving to database management, catalog maintenance, reference, retrospective conversion, and more.

Library Management Systems
400 Corporate Pointe
Culver City, CA 90230
www.lrms.com

The Library Management Systems (LMS) has been providing library staffing, recruitment, and consulting to public and special libraries and businesses since 1983. LMS organizes and manages special libraries and designs and implements major projects, including retrospective conversions, automation studies, and records management. It also performs high-quality cataloging outsourcing and furnishes contract staffing to all categories of information centers. LMS has a large database of librarians and library assistants on call for long- and short-term projects and provides permanent placement at all levels.

Medical Library Association
65 East Wacker Place, Suite 1900
Chicago, IL 60601
www.mlanet.org

MLA News is a monthly newsletter that lists positions wanted and positions available. All listings for positions available must give a minimum salary, and a salary range is preferred. The Medical Library Association also offers a placement service at its annual meeting each spring. Job advertisements received for the *MLA News* publication are posted to the MLANET jobline during the month of the issue date.

Music Library Association
8551 Research Way, Suite 180
Middleton, WI 53562
www.musiclibraryassoc.org

Career resources as well as a job placement service that lists jobs in academic, public, performing arts, orchestra, conservatory, media, or radio libraries are available on the Music Library Association website.

Pro Libra Associate
436 Springfield Avenue, Suite 3
Summit, NJ 07901
www.prolibra.com

A multiservice library firm, Pro Libra specializes in permanent and temporary personnel placement, consulting, management, and project support for libraries and information centers. For more than twenty-five years, it has provided personnel services to catalog, inventory, and staff libraries and information centers in corporate, academic, and public institutions.

REFORMA, National Association to Promote Library Service to
　　the Spanish-Speaking
P.O. Box 4386
Fresno, CA 93744
www.reforma.org

Employers wishing to do direct mailings to the REFORMA membership (nine hundred plus) may obtain mailing labels arranged by zip code. Job ads also are published quarterly in the *REFORMA Newsletter*. Job openings may also be posted on the REFORMA website free of charge.

Society of American Archivists
17 North State Street, Suite 1425
Chicago, IL 60602
www.archivists.org

The Archival Outlook newsletter is sent to members six times annually and contains features about the archival profession and other timely pieces on courses in archival administration, meetings, and professional opportunities. The *Online Employment Bulletin* is a weekly listing of professional opportunities posted on the website.

Special Libraries Association
331 South Patrick Street
Alexandria, VA 22314
www.sla.org

Resources and career links are available online, and most Special Libraries Association (SLA) chapters have employment chairpersons who make referrals for employers and job seekers. Several SLA chapters have joblines. The association's monthly magazine, *Information Outlook*, carries classified advertising. SLA offers an employment clearinghouse and career advisory service during its annual conference, held in June, and also provides a discount to members using the résumé-evaluation service.

TeleSec CORESTAFF
815 Connecticut Avenue NW, Suite 350
Washington, DC 20006
www.corestaff.com/searchlines

TeleSec CORESTAFF is a division of CORESTAFF Services, a professional staffing service resource for leading companies throughout the region with online links for employers and job seekers. A variety of opportunities include direct hire, temporary, temp-to-hire, and contract positions. Positions are in the major federal agencies, law firms, corporations, associations, and academic institutions. TeleSec CORESTAFF has been a leader in the staffing industry since its founding in 1948. Check its website for library openings and register online.

Tuft and Associates
1209 Astor Street
Chicago, IL 60610
www.tuftassoc.com

Tuft and Associates specialize in nationwide executive searches for administrative posts in libraries and information centers.

Wontawk
25 West Forty-Third Street, Suite 812
New York, NY 10036
www.wontawk.com

Nationwide direct hire, temporary, and temp-to-hire positions are listed online for professional, paraprofessional, and support services for all levels of responsibility and all skills.

State Library Agencies and Associations

Most state and regional library associations provide online lists of job openings. A comprehensive list of these associations can be found on the American Library Association website, alphabetized by state. These detailed listings include contact information and journals for each state's association. When vacancy postings are available, state library newsletters or journals will often list them. In addition, some library agencies also provide job listings. Some of these resources are included below, along with other resources for each state. To get a current and comprehensive listing, visit www.ala.org. Most of these sites provide links to job postings.

Alabama Library Association—allanet.org
Alaska Library Association—www.akla.org
Arizona Library Association—www.azla.org
Arkansas Library Association—www.arlib.org
California Library Association—www.cla-net.org
Colorado Association of Libraries—http://cal-webs.org
Colorado State Library Jobline—www.cde.state.co.us/
cdelib/slsvcs.htm
Connecticut Library Association—www.ctlibrary
association.org
Connecticut Library Jobline—www.ctilibrarians.org/
ctlibs/jobs.html
Delaware Library Association—www2.lib.udel.edu/dla
District of Columbia Library Association—www.dcla.org
Florida Library Association—www.flalib.org
Florida Library Jobs—www.floridalibraryjobs.org
Georgia Library Association—http://gla.georgia
libraries.org or www.lisjobs.com/states/georgia.htm
Hawaii Library Association—http://ohana.chaminade
.edu/hla
Idaho Commission for Libraries—www.libraries.idaho.gov
Idaho Library Association—www.idaholibraries.org
Illinois Library Association—www.ila.org

Indiana Library Federation—www.ilfonline.org

Iowa Library Association—www.iowalibrary
association.org

Kansas Library Association—http://skyways.lib
.ks.us/KLA

Kentucky Library Association—www.kylibasn.org or the
library job hotline at www.kdla.ky.gov/libsupport/
jobline.htm

Louisiana Library Association—www.llaonline.org

Maine Library Association—mainelibraries.org

Maryland Library Association—www.mdlib.org

Massachusetts Library Association—www.masslib.org or
the Board of Library Commissioners at www.mlin.lib
.ma.us

Michigan Library Association Jobline—www.mla.lib.mi.us

Minnesota Library Association—www.mnlibrary
association.org

Mississippi Library Association—www.misslib.org

Missouri Library Association—molib.org

Montana Library Association—www.mtlib.org

Nebraska Library Association—www.nebraska
libraries.org

Nevada Library Association—www.nevadalibraries.org

New Hampshire Library Association—www.nh
librarians.org

New Hampshire State Library—www.nh.gov/nhsl/
services/librarians/employment.html

New Jersey Library Association—www.njla.org

New Mexico Library Association—www.nmla.org

New York Library Association—www.nyla.org

North Carolina Library Association—www.nclaonline.org
or statelibrary.dcr.state.nc.us/jobs/jobs.htm
North Dakota Library Association—www.ndla.info
Ohio Library Council—www.olc.org
Oklahoma Library Association—www.oklibs.org or the
Department of Libraries Jobline at www.odl.state.ok.us/
fyi/jobline/jobokla.htm
Oregon Library Association—www.olaweb.org
Oregon State Library Jobline—www.oregon.gov/OSL/
jobs.shtml
Pennsylvania Library Association—www.palibraries.org
Rhode Island Library Association—www.rilibraryassoc.org
South Carolina Library Association—www.scla.org
South Dakota Library Association—www.sdlibrary
association.org
Tennessee Library Association—www.tnla.org
Texas Library Association—www.txla.org
Texas State Library Jobline—www.tsl.state.tx.us/ld/jobs
Utah Library Association—www.ula.org
Vermont Library Association—www.vermontlibraries.org
Virginia Library Association—www.vla.org or the Library
of Virginia at www.lva.lib.va.us/whoweare/jobs
Washington Library Association—www.wla.org
West Virginia Library Association—wvla.org
Wisconsin Library Association—www.wla.lib.wi.us
Wyoming Library Association—www.wyla.org

Although they may not have formal placement services, many
state library agencies will refer applicants informally when vacancies are known to exist.

Regional Library Associations

Regional library associations often will make referrals, run ads in association newsletters, or operate a placement service at annual conferences in addition to the joblines sponsored by some groups. Although listings are infrequent, job vacancies are often placed in newsletters or journals when available. For a complete listing of journals and their publication schedules, along with the states covered by each region, visit the American Library Association website at www.ala.org. Regional library associations include the following:

Mountain Plains Library Association—www.mpla.us
New England Library Association—www.nelib.org
Pacific Northwest Library Association—www.pnla.org
Southeastern Library Association—sela.jsu.edu

The following state and regional library associations have indicated some type of placement service or job help or search service, although it may only be held at annual conferences: Alabama, California, Connecticut, Georgia, Idaho, Indiana, Iowa, Kansas, Kentucky, Louisiana, Maryland, Massachusetts, New England, New Jersey, New York, North Carolina, Ohio, Oregon, Pacific Northwest, Pennsylvania, South Dakota, Southeastern, Tennessee, Texas, Vermont, Wisconsin, and Wyoming.

Library and Information Studies Programs

Library and information studies programs offer some type of service for their current students as well as for alumni. Most schools provide job-hunting and résumé-writing seminars. Many have outside speakers representing different types of libraries or recent graduates relating career experiences. Faculty or a designated placement officer offers individual advising services or critiquing of résumés. For ALA-accredited library and information studies programs, check with your individual college/university to see what placement activities it covers. You can also go to the ALA website (ala.org) at its Web page entitled "Guide to Employment Sources in the Library and Information Sciences" (www.ala.org/ala/hrdr/ libraryempre sources/guideemployment.cfm).

In addition to job vacancy postings, some schools issue printed listings, operate joblines, have electronic access to job information, or provide various database services. Check with your individual college/university to discover what resources and opportunities it has available. Here are some additional listings for job placement information:

> Albany—send message to Listserv@cnsibm.albany.edu to subscribe; job placement bulletin is free to School of Information Science and Policy (SISP) students
>
> Alberta—www.bcla.bc.ca/jobs/index.html
>
> Arizona—send subscription message to listserv@listserv.ari zona.edu
>
> British Columbia—uses BCLA Jobline, (604) 683-5354 or (800) 661-1445; uses BCLA jobpage at www.bcla.bc.ca/ jobs/index.html
>
> Buffalo—job postings for alumni: send message to sils-l @listserv.acsu.buffalo.edu; for students: ubmls-l@list serv.acsu.buffalo.edu
>
> Clarion—www.clarion.edu/student/career/jobs/index.htm
>
> Dalhousie—Listserv for Atlantic Canada jobs, send message to mailserv@ac.dal.ca

Dominican— publishes *Placement News* every two weeks
(free for six months following graduation; then $15 per
year for students and $25 for alumni and others)

Drexel—www.cis.drexel.edu/placement/placement.html

Emporia—has weekly bulletin for school, university, and
public jobs and a separate bulletin for special
jobsIllinois—in partnership with Indiana and
Washington, offers free online placement JOBSearch
database available on campus and via access through
telnet alexia.lis.uiuc.edu; login: jobs; password: Urbaign;
or carousel.lis.uiuc.edu/~jobs

Indiana—www.slis.indiana.edu/cfdocs/slisjobs

Iowa—www.uiowa.edu/homepage/employers/index.html

Kentucky—www.uky.edu/CommInfoStudies/SLIS/
jobs.htm

Maryland—Listserv@umdd.umd.edu to subscribe

Michigan—www.si.umich.edu/jobfinder

Missouri—www.coe.missouri.edu

North Carolina at Chapel Hill—e-mail: listproc@ils.unc
.edu to subscribe or ils.unc.edu/ils/web/listservs.html

Pittsburgh—www.sis.pitt.edu/~lsdept/libjobs.htm

Rutgers—www.scils.rutgers.edu or scils-jobs@scils.rutgers
.edu

Simmons—www.simmons.edu/gslis/jobline.html; operates
New England Jobline, which announces professional
vacancies

South Carolina—www.libsci.sc.edu/career/job.htm

South Florida—in cooperation with the ALIS organization

Southern Connecticut—www.scsu.ctstateu.edu; printed
listing twice a month, mailed to students/alumni free

St. John's—lists job postings for United States, Canada, and abroad; send notices to libis@stjohns.edu

Syracuse—lists selected jobs online through electronic mail to students

Texas Woman's—www.twu.edu/o-cs/home.html

Toronto—www.fis.utoronto.ca/resources/jobsite

Washington—send notices to slis@u.washington.edu

Western Ontario—www.fims.uwo.ca/lis/employment .html

Wisconsin–Madison—now sends listings from Wisconsin and Minnesota to Illinois for JOBSearch

Wisconsin–Milwaukee—Listserv@slis.uwm.edu to subscribe; www.slis.uwm.edu/MLIS_Jobs/MLIS_Job _Links.htm

Employers often will list jobs with schools only in their particular geographical area; some library schools will give information to non-alumni regarding their specific locales, but they are not staffed to handle mail requests, and advice is usually given in person. Check with your school to determine if it will allow librarians in its areas to view listings.

You can request a list of accredited program addresses and phone numbers from the ALA or check in the *Bowker Annual.* Individuals interested in placement services of other library education programs should contact those schools directly.

Federal Employment Information Sources

Consideration for employment in many federal libraries requires establishing Civil Service eligibility. Although the actual job search is your responsibility, the Office of Personnel Management (OPM)

has developed the USAJOBS website www.usajobs.opm.gov to assist you. The website also has an online résumé-builder feature for job seekers to create online résumés specifically designed for applying for federal jobs.

USA Jobs Touch Screen Computer is a computer-based system utilizing touch screen technology. These kiosks, located throughout the nation in OPM offices, federal office buildings, and other locations, allow you to access current worldwide federal job opportunities, online information, and more.

Applicants should attempt to make personal contact directly with the federal agencies in which they are interested. This is essential in the Washington, DC, area, where more than half the vacancies occur. Most librarian positions are in three agencies: Army, Navy, and Veterans Administration.

Some excepted service agencies are not required to hire through the usual OPM channels. Although these agencies may require the standard forms, they maintain their own employee selection policies and procedures. Government establishments with positions outside the competitive Civil Service include the following:

Board of Governors of the Federal Reserve System
Central Intelligence Agency
Defense Intelligence Agency
Department of Medicine and Surgery
Federal Bureau of Investigation
Foreign Service of the United States
General Accounting Office
International Monetary Fund
Judicial Branch
Legislative Branch

Library of Congress
National Science Foundation
National Security Agency
Organizations of American States
Pan American Health Organization
Tennessee Valley Authority
United Nations Secretariat
U.S. Mission to the United Nations
U.S. Nuclear Regulatory Commission
U.S. Postal Service
World Bank

The Library of Congress, which is the world's largest and most comprehensive library, is an excepted-service agency in the legislative branch and administers its own independent merit-selection system. Job classifications, pay, and benefits are the same as in other federal agencies, and qualification requirements generally correspond to those used by the U.S. Office of Personnel Management. The library does not use registers but announces vacancies as they become available. A separate application must be submitted for each vacancy announcement. For most professional positions, announcements are widely distributed and open for a minimum of thirty days. Qualification requirements and ranking criteria are stated on the vacancy announcement, and job openings can be searched on the Web at www.loc.gov/hr/employment/index.php. The Library of Congress Human Resources Operations Office is located at:

James Madison Memorial Building
101 Independence Avenue SE
Washington, DC 20540

Additional General and Specialized Job Sources

In addition to these sources, you can find additional information through indirect, though equally important, sources, such as the following:

Affirmative Action Register
225 South Meramec Avenue, Suite 400
St. Louis, MO 63105
www.aarjobs.com

The *Affirmative Action Register (AAR)* is a national magazine and website that connects employers to professionals seeking jobs. For more than thirty years, it has served individuals regardless of race, color, national origin, religion, gender, age, sexual preference, or disability. *AAR Magazine* is distributed free of charge to certain organizations and locations, and permission is granted to reproduce copies of the magazine for further distribution. For more information, visit the AAR website.

The magazine bulletin is offered to: leading businesses; industrial and academic institutions; more than four thousand agencies that recruit qualified minorities and women; all known female, minority, and handicapped professional organizations, placement offices, newspapers, magazines, and rehabilitation facilities; and more than eight thousand federal, state, and local governmental employment units with a total readership in excess of 3.5 million. Individual mail subscriptions are available, and librarian listings are found in most issues and are sent free to libraries on request.

The Chronicle of Higher Education
1255 Twenty-Third Street NW, Seventh Floor
Washington, DC 20037
www.chronicle.com/jobs

Published in print weekly, with breaks in August and December, and weekdays online, the *Chronicle* lists a variety of library positions, including administrative and faculty jobs. Job listings are searchable by specific categories, keywords, or geographic locations.

School librarians often find that the channels for locating positions in education are of more value than the channels for locating library positions (for example, contacting county or city school superintendent offices). Another excellent resource is each university's placement office, which carries listings for a variety of school-system jobs. A list of commercial teacher agencies can be accessed by going to www.jobsforteachers.com.

Overseas

Opportunities for employment in foreign countries are limited, and immigration policies of individual countries should be investigated. Employment for Americans is virtually limited to U.S. government libraries, libraries of U.S. firms doing worldwide business, and American schools abroad. Library journals from other countries will sometimes list vacancy notices. Some persons have obtained jobs by contacting foreign publishers or vendors directly. Non-U.S. government jobs usually call for foreign language fluency. Librarian job postings found at http://bubl.ac.uk are a listing of U.S. and foreign jobs collected by the Bulletin Board for Libraries.

The following four resources will help you find work as a lecturer through the Department of Defense overseas (in some cases), or through the Peace Corps.

Council for International Exchange of Scholars (CIES)
3007 Tilden Street NW, Suite 5L
Washington, DC 20008
www.cies.org

The Council for International Exchange of Scholars (CIES) administers U.S. government Fulbright awards for university lecturing and advanced research abroad; usually ten to fifteen awards per year are made to U.S. citizens who are specialists in library or information sciences. In addition, many countries offer awards in any specialization of research or lecturing for which specialists in library and information science may apply. Lecturing awards usually require university or college teaching experience. Several opportunities also exist for professional librarians. Applications and information may be obtained, beginning in March each year, from CIES. The worldwide application deadline is August 1.

Department of Defense Education Activity
4040 North Fairfax Drive, Webb Building
Arlington, VA 22203
www.dodea.edu

The Department of Defense Education Activity (DoDEA) has overall management and operational responsibilities for the education of dependent children of active-duty U.S. military personnel and DoD civilians who are stationed in foreign areas. The schools are operated on military installations for the children of U.S. military and civilian personnel stationed overseas. It is also responsible for teacher recruitment. For a complete application brochure, write to it or find career opportunities by visiting its website, which provides information on educator employment opportunities in more than 167 schools worldwide.

International Schools Services
15 Roszel Road
Princeton, NJ 08543
www.iss.edu

The International Schools Services (ISS) is a private, not-for-profit organization founded in 1955 to serve American schools overseas that are other than Department of Defense schools. These are American, international elementary and secondary schools enrolling the children of business and diplomatic families living abroad. ISS services to overseas schools include recruitment and recommendation of personnel, curricular and administrative guidance, purchasing, facility planning, and more. ISS publishes a comprehensive directory of overseas schools as well as a bimonthly newsletter, *NewsLinks*, for those interested in the intercultural educational community. You may obtain information regarding these publications and other services by writing to it or by visiting its website.

Peace Corps
1111 Twentieth Street NW
Washington, DC 20526
www.peacecorps.gov

Volunteer opportunities exist for those with an M.A./M.S. or B.A./B.S. in library science and one year of related work experience and is available for a two-year tour of duty to U.S. citizens only. Living allowance, health care, transportation, and other benefits are provided. Visit the Peace Corps website for more information.

Search Associates
www.search-associates.com

Search Associates is a private organization of former overseas school directors who organize recruitment fairs to place teachers, librarians, and administrators in independent, K–12 schools around the world. These accredited schools, based on the American model, range in size from fewer than forty to more than four thousand students. They serve the children of diplomats and businesspeople from dozens of countries and offer highly attractive personal and professional opportunities for experienced librarians.

Exchange Programs

For students wishing to work at overseas libraries, the following two organizations will aid in library exchanges, mostly in Great Britain:

International Federation of Library Associations and Institutions
P.O. Box 95312
2509 CH The Hague
Netherlands
www.ifla.org

Most exchanges are handled by direct negotiation between interested parties. A few libraries have established exchange programs for their own staffs. To facilitate exchange arrangements, the *IFLA Journal* (published four times a year) lists persons who wish to exchange positions with someone outside their own country. All listings must include the following: full name, address, present position, qualifications (and year obtained), language abilities, preferred country/city/library, and type of position. For more information on available positions, visit www.LibrarianExchange.net or go to www.EducatorExchange.com.

LIBEX Bureau for International Staff Exchange
Thomas Parry Library
University of Wales Aberystwyth
Llanbadarn Fawr, Aberystwyth
Ceredigion SY23 3AS
Wales, United Kingdom
www.cilip.org.uk/jobscareers/libex

The LIBEX Bureau for International Staff Exchange assists in exchanges for British librarians who wish to work abroad and for librarians from the United States, Canada, European Economic Community, and other countries who wish to undertake exchanges as well.

Using Information Skills in Nonlibrary Settings

A great deal of interest exists in using information skills in a variety of ways in nonlibrary settings. These jobs are not usually found through the regular library placement sources, although many library and information studies programs are trying to generate such listings for their students and alumni. Job listings that do exist may not call specifically for librarians, so ingenuity may be needed to search out jobs where information management skills are needed.

You can work on a freelance basis by offering services to businesses, alternative schools, community agencies, legislators, and so on; these opportunities are not usually found in advertisements but are created by developing contacts and publicity over a period of time. A number of information-brokering business firms have developed from individual freelance experiences. Small companies or other organizations often need one-time service for organizing files or collections, bibliographic research for special projects, indexing or abstracting, compilation of directories, and consulting services. Bibliographic networks and online database companies use librarians as information managers, trainers, researchers, systems and database analysts, online services managers, and so on. Jobs in this area are sometimes found in library network newsletters or data processing journals.

Some librarians work in law firms as litigation case supervisors, organizing and analyzing records needed for specific legal cases, and with publishers as sales representatives. They can also act as marketing directors, editors, and computer services experts and with community agencies as adult education coordinators, volunteer administrators, and grant writers.

Classifieds in both *Publishers Weekly* and *The National Business Employment Weekly* may lead to information-related positions. You might consider reading the Sunday classified ad sections in metropolitan newspapers in their entirety to locate descriptions calling for information skills but under a variety of job titles.

Burwell Enterprises
5619 Plumtree Drive
Dallas, TX 75252
www.burwellinc.com

The Burwell World Directory of Information Brokers is an annual publication that lists information brokers, freelance librarians, independent information specialists, and institutions that provide services for a fee. There is a minimal charge for an annual listing, and the *Burwell Directory Online* is searchable free on the Internet at www.burwellinc.com. Print and CD-ROM versions are available. Also published is a bimonthly newsletter, *Information Broker*, which includes articles by, for, and about individuals and companies in the fee-based information field; book reviews; calendar of upcoming events; and issue-oriented articles. A bibliography and other publications on the field of information brokering also are available.

Association of Independent Information Professionals
www.aaip.org

You can obtain classifieds through the Association of Independent Information Professionals, which was formed for individuals who own and operate for-profit information companies.

A growing number of publications are addressing opportunities for librarians in the broader information arena.

American Society of Indexers
10200 West Forty-Fourth Avenue, Suite 304
Wheat Ridge, CO 80033
www.asindexing.org

The American Society of Indexers has a number of publications that would be useful for individuals who are interested in indexing.

Temporary/Part-Time Positions

You may consider working as a substitute librarian or in temporary positions as an alternative career path or as an interim step while looking for a regular job. This type of work can provide valuable contacts and experience. Organizations that hire library workers for part-time or temporary jobs include:

Advanced Information Management
444 Castro Street, Suite 320
Mountain View, CA 94041

or

900 Wilshire Boulevard, Suite 1424
Los Angeles, CA 90017

C. Berger Group
327 East Gundersen Drive
Carol Stream, IL 60188

Gossage Regan Associates
25 West Forty-Third Street
New York, NY 10036

Information Management Division
1160 Veirs Mill Road, Suite 414
Wheaton, MD 20902

The Library Co-Op
3840 Park Avenue, Suite 107
Edison, NJ 08820

Library Management Systems
Corporate Pointe, Suite 755
Culver City, CA 9023

Library Management Systems
Three Bethesda Metro Center, Suite 700
Bethesda, MD 20814

Pro Libra Associates
6 Inwood Place
Maplewood, NJ 07040

Wontawk Gossage Associates
304 Newbury Street
Boston, MA 02115

Part-time jobs are not always advertised but can be found by canvassing local libraries and leaving applications.

Job Hunting in General

The skills of librarians can be applied in traditional library settings and wherever information needs to be organized and presented in an effective, efficient, and service-oriented fashion. However, it will take a considerable investment of time, energy, imagination, and money before a satisfying position is created or obtained in a conventional library or another type of information service. Usually, no one method or source of job hunting can be used alone.

Public and school library certification requirements often vary from state to state; contact the particular state library agency for such information. Certification requirements are summarized in *Certification of Public Librarians in the United States*, fourth edition (1991), from the ALA Office for Human Resource Development and Recruitment.

A summary of school library/media certification requirements by state is found in *Requirements for Certification of Teachers, Counselors, Librarians, and Administrators for Elementary and Secondary Schools*, which is published annually by the University of Chicago Press. State supervisors of school library media services also may be contacted for information on specific states.

Civil Service requirements either on a local, county, or state level often add another layer of procedures to the job search. Some Civil Service jurisdictions require written and/or oral examinations; others assign a ranking based on a review of credentials. Jobs are usually filled from the top candidates on a qualified list of applicants. Because the exams are held only at certain times and a variety of jobs may be filled from a single list of applicants (for example, all Librarian I positions regardless of type of function), check to see if the library you are interested in falls under Civil Service procedures.

If you want a position in a specific subject area or in a particular geographical location, remember those reference skills to ferret information from directories and other tools regarding local industries, schools, subject collections, and so on. Directories such as the *American Library Directory*, *Subject Collections*, *Directory of Special Libraries and Information Centers*, and *Directory of Federal Libraries*, as well as state directories or directories of other special subject areas, provide a wealth of information for job seekers. Some state employment offices will include library listings as part of their job services department.

Some students pool resources to hire a clipping service to get classified librarian ads for a particular geographical area. Interesting sources in library literature include the following:

- Ballard, Terry. "We're Honored That You Applied Here." *Information Today*, v. 15–2, February 1998, p. 42.
- Fox, Charlie. "Employment and Job Search." *Library Mosaics*, v. 10–3, May/June 1999, pp. 5–19.
- Roberts, Joni R. "Have I Got A Job For You." *Library Mosaics*, v. 10–3, May/June 1999, pp. 14–15.

Another Internet source is www.careerpath.com. For information on other job-hunting and personnel matters, contact the following:

ALA Office for Human Resource
    Development and Recruitment
50 East Huron Street
Chicago, IL 60611
www.ala.org

Salaries, Status, Tenure, Retirement, and Related Benefits

Recently, there has been greater emphasis placed on the benefits offered by a particular position than on its salary. These benefits may include hospitalization and other medical insurance, retirement plans, house-finding assistance, and aid in negotiating the purchase of a home. For an initial appointment and for a change of positions, it is important to determine the various benefits of the job and to set up a way to compare the different programs at different libraries or information centers.

Salaries

In thinking about salaries, it is useful to have an idea of the salary range for people with similar qualifications in similar positions. You must recognize, however, that no two people are exactly alike or exactly comparable in those terms. Sources of information about reasonable expectations may be placement counselors, surveys of salaries—such as the one for beginning positions that has appeared annually in *Library Journal*—and advertisements for positions that list a salary range.

In evaluating a salary, it may be useful to compare it with the actual take-home pay received during each pay period. The pattern of pay periods can be important, too; if you are accustomed to being paid every other week, you may find it difficult to adjust to monthly payments or vice versa. The amount of state income tax withheld and other deductions, such as dues in a staff association or union, can have considerable effect on the ratio of take-home pay to actual earnings. In comparing positions in two different locations, you need to consider the relative costs of living. If a car is required for the job but not supplied by the library or information center, if circumstances require a lengthy commute, or if evening hours require additional amounts for food or transportation, you should figure those costs and their impact on the salary offered.

It is wise to obtain a salary schedule, if available, and to note your place on it; also note possible opportunities for advancement. Information about when and how salary increments are made should be obtained as early as possible. In fact, you should verify all benefits information before actually committing yourself to a permanent position.

Actual salaries of librarians and information scientists are difficult to pinpoint because of the diversity of settings in which these people work. Regional differences may mean that very different salaries are paid for the same position. Although a beginning librarian may start in the low twenties per year, the director of a large academic library may earn more than six figures.

One sector of library employment where good data are available is that of new graduates from schools accredited by the American Library Association. Information is provided annually in *Library Journal*, which reports salary by type of placement and region.

Another way to discover current regional salaries is to peruse job announcements in periodicals such as *Library Journal* or *American Libraries*. Visit joblist.ala.org for a list of employment opportunities. This free service will allow you to search current job openings or post a résumé for employers to review, but you will need to create an account first. The American Library Association and the American Professional Association (ALA-APA), in conjunction with the ALA Office for Research and Statistics, now publishes two annual salary surveys, which are available from the ALA's online store. The most current surveys available at the time of publication were the *ALA-APA Salary Survey 2006: Librarian—Public and Academic* and the *ALA-APA Salary Survey 2006: MLS—Public and Academic*. These surveys contain data from more than one thousand public and academic libraries on more than ten thousand individual salaries at state and regional levels. In 2006, these surveys reflected a mean salary of $50,976, with salaries ranging from $22,000 to $253,500.

According to the *Occupational Outlook Handbook*, a publication of the U.S. Bureau of Labor Statistics, salaries of librarians vary according to the individual's qualifications and the type, size, and location of the library. Librarians with primarily administrative duties often have greater earnings.

Median annual earnings of librarians in 2006, the latest figures that are currently available, were $49,060. The middle 50 percent earned between $39,250 and $60,800. The lowest 10 percent earned less than $30,930, and the highest 10 percent earned more than $74,670.

Median annual earnings in the industries employing the largest numbers of librarians in 2006 were as follows:

- Junior colleges: $52,030
- Colleges, universities, and professional schools: $51,160
- Elementary and secondary schools: $50,710
- Local government: $44,960
- Other information services: $44,170

In 2007, the average annual salary for all librarians in the federal government in nonsupervisory, supervisory, and managerial positions was $80,873.

Status and Tenure

Salaries may be only one small part of the benefits package. The employee's status and the status of other employees in the library and information services areas of an institution also should be verified. The most frequently discussed benefits issue related to academic libraries is whether faculty status is given to professional employees in the library. Usually, this status means that individual employees are placed on salary scales comparable or equal to those of the teaching faculty. Academic rank (such as professor, associate professor) may be assigned; requirements for advancement and tenure may be set for faculty library staff members on a basis similar to that for other faculty. If you are considering appointment in an academic library, find out what the present status of librarians is, whether there are any efforts underway that are likely to change it, and what the prospects are for advancement or simply for continuing an appointment at that institution.

There may be other aspects to status. Customarily, you should expect to be employed at the level for which you are academically prepared, with experience a part of the consideration. This assumes that as a professional person you will receive a professional appointment, unless exceptional circumstances lead you to accept a different kind of assignment. In that case, obtain a clear understanding of your responsibilities in terms of remaining in the position a set period of time and of the employer's position regarding a possible future opportunity or change of status.

Tenure, as generally related to personnel matters, refers to the benefit that ensures that you will be retained permanently in the current position or in a comparable one, except for unusual causes. These causes may be conviction of a crime; exceptional loss of revenue to the employing institution, thus requiring drastic reduction of personnel; or similar situations. Tenure customarily is granted only after a specified period of employment because it commits the institution to a long-term agreement in which the employee is relatively free to leave but the institution is not as free to dismiss the employee. In academic libraries and school libraries, tenure is a customary benefit, but it must be earned. Remember that tenure usually is offered in terms of general employment, not in terms of a specific position. Thus, in a school library, tenure may protect you when curtailment of funds reduces the library program, but you may have to accept a position as a teacher to remain in a professional position in the school district.

The benefit of tenure is nearly unknown in special libraries, where competition for excellence may be deliberately encouraged. It is possible that every staff member will attempt to show her or his value, with job security an uncommon benefit for all personnel. Some public libraries have a kind of tenure system in which staff members are considered permanent after a set period of time, but it is subject to the same kinds of pressures as exist in other, more formal systems.

Retirement

The retirement plans of various libraries and information centers vary. There are also policies about the terms of retirement that should be known to all employees. For example, is early retirement—before age sixty-five, for example—encouraged? Is it possible? Is there an age for mandatory retirement? Is there provision for retirement based on disability? Are there any benefits available to retired staff members, for example, use of the library's facilities and staff? Although it may seem that questions about retirement are of major interest to older staff members only, everyone should be interested in them. This is because they may seem more relevant to the individual and because the library's attitude toward its retired staff members may be an indication of the value and interest it associates with all employees.

Social Security retirement benefits usually are available to public employees. Working people contribute a portion of their salaries, withheld at the time they are paid; employers also contribute a similar amount, with both parts going toward a fund that will provide retirement benefits to the individual. Other benefits associated with Social Security are provisions for allotments to surviving spouses and children in the event of an employee's death. In most instances, the amount Social Security will pay at retirement is so small that other retirement plans must be implemented.

To provide the kind of financial security most people will need in retirement, many employers require participation in plans similar to Social Security. The employee contributes a set amount of her or his income; and the employing institution supplements that with a matching or similar amount. Sometimes the employing institution may pay all of an employee's contribution to the plan, but such other benefits as salary may be proportionally lower.

State retirement or pension plans, municipal employee plans, and national plans such as Teachers Insurance and Annuity Association include large numbers of employees, thus usually ensuring good financial management of the pension funds. The national plans may offer the additional advantage of permitting you to remain in the same plan without remaining at the institution. The chief values of these retirement plans are that they enforce regular saving, provide a supplement to the employer's contributions, and provide for some mobility without loss of benefits.

Related Benefits

Other kinds of benefits may be numerous and difficult to determine in value. Credit union membership may be available to library personnel, providing another encouragement to save and a possible source of loans. Hospitalization and other kinds of health insurance also may be offered, sometimes with the employer paying a major part of the premiums. Be sure you check the different kinds of health insurance, the arrangements for payment of premiums, and the length of time before you become eligible for benefits. These are important matters to consider, especially when changing positions.

Some employers offer free or reduced tuition. At an institution of higher education, the benefit may be extended to the employee's children or spouse, either at that institution or at a comparable one. Full or partial reimbursement for tuition for courses taken is more common in other kinds of libraries. If there are stipulations to these educational benefits, it is usually your responsibility to meet whatever requirements are set.

Other fringe benefits may include reimbursement of travel expenses for professional meetings or conferences, payment of dues in professional associations, or provision of assets such as professional books or periodicals. One unstated benefit may be employee access to resources in a library or information center. Your personal research interests may be served in this way, and you may avoid fees charged for using some collections.

The benefits category is broad and includes more than those discussed here. Decisions about benefits are personal ones, but information about their availability is generally well publicized. Be sure to find out about the benefits available and use them intelligently.

5

Future of the Information Professions

Management of information is a growth profession. Governments, universities, corporations, and schools are acquiring and using information at greater rates than at any time in the past. The advent of electronic publishing enables individuals to connect with vast databases and the Internet through a computer in their home offices. Telecommunications make it possible to transmit data and e-mail to colleagues instantaneously.

However, the huge amount of easily obtained information overwhelms the average individual. Businesses and universities could not cope with the masses of information available without the services of a skilled information manager. Regardless of the type of institution in which information professionals choose to work—libraries, information centers, archives, or database firms—the need for their skills will continue to increase.

Developing models of libraries of the future includes an emphasis on technology to dissolve limitations and enhance the idea of the learning society. The future of the library is best imagined from the point of view of the user rather than any of the structural components that might be assembled to provide service. From this vantage point, the evolution from paper library to automated library to electronic library is simply a continuum of better mechanisms to respond to end-user needs. But what drives librarians to maintain professional domination over information provided to users is not merely the mastery of technology or the facilitation of collaborative partnerships, but the librarians' vision of equal access for all.

Digitization, as exemplified by the Library of Congress National Digital Library Program, is changing the way we store and retrieve information. For example, the Library of Congress has digitized millions of items, including Revolutionary War maps, handwritten drafts of the Declaration of Independence and the Gettysburg Address, and personal papers of the first twenty-three U.S. presidents. The oversight of this scope of preservation is simply one of the ways in which the role of information professionals has been changing over the last decade.

The simultaneous development of digitized information storage and delivery and a growing and pervasive commitment to a learning society positions library and information professionals to use technology. While we can imagine users shifting from working with librarians providing service from a library to working with librarians who facilitate access from a terminal, can our users imagine the same? A simple analogy might answer this question. Over the last decade or so, shopping online has escalated as a way in which many people acquire goods. For these fairly focused consumers, the experience of browsing, looking, and interacting is less important than expediency. Yet traditional stores continue to provide goods to consumers who may have no phone, may have no credit cards, or may simply be disinclined to place convenience over other objective experiences. Will we see the demise of the marketplace as it is configured today? Most likely not, as many individuals view purchasing as a more complex set of activities than simply acquiring merchandise. In much the same way, there are information seekers who see the physical library itself as important and value it as a place to obtain discrete information.

As suburban sprawl and the hectic demands of daily life impose higher levels of stress and aimlessness, the library will remain a cultural institution in which vast amounts of information are stored in an orderly fashion.

This is not to say that the evolution of the virtual library will not continue or that it will not engage a larger and larger market share of users. The library as a physical place where individuals go for human assistance will likely coexist over the next twenty years.

The future of careers in the information profession is one of excitement, integration of new technologies, and the inspired commitment to preserve the record of human achievement and make it available to all. Here we discuss other important concerns for information professionals.

Intellectual Freedom

One of the proudest traditions of American librarianship has been its defense of intellectual freedom. Simply stated, this usually has been closely related to issues about selection and use of library materials, requiring that libraries have the freedom to give users access to all kinds of materials without regard for the pressures that may be exerted by special-interest groups to limit the provision of books, journals, and other materials.

In more recent years, concern for an individual's privacy has led to new problems of intellectual freedom. Any agency that is concerned with information and its acquisition and storage is likely to collect material that is of special value to some outside agency. This may be the result of research that could be extremely valuable to a corporation other than the one that initiated it, or it could be information that others want on the reading (or at least the book borrowing) habits of an individual. Conflicts exist between the long tradition of libraries and information centers to provide information freely and preserve the privacy rights of individuals and their obligations to serve the agency that funds or controls them.

One may expect that these complicated questions will become more complex and numerous over time. If you are entering a career in the information field, it is important for you to have clear principles of your own. You will also need a clear understanding of the requirements of your work and of the need to deal with these issues in a reasonable, ethical way.

Social Responsibility and Information Equity

Though there has never been a question that libraries and information centers have a responsibility to society, in recent years the term *social responsibility* has come to have special significance. It refers to the need to provide fair service to all, to employ people on an equitable basis, to represent minority groups among employees, and to take a stand on public issues. In some instances, confusion and conflict may occur between defending intellectual freedom and defending social responsibility. The former suggests openness to the provision of all information, and the latter suggests emphasis on a particular point of view.

An interesting example of this conflict occurs, for example, when selection of materials for children's collections deals with the problem of how females and males are presented in media for children. The idea that girls are weak while boys are strong or that girls are stay-at-home types while boys are adventurers conflicts with many people's beliefs. Numerous children's books and other media suggest or firmly state that idea. Those who believe in presentation of truly fair and equal gender roles have strongly supported removing biased media from library collections. Strong support exists for close cooperation with publishers and producers to eliminate such stereotyped presentations. Similarly, strong support exists for the idea that such pressure is in violation of intellectual freedom and is closely allied with, if not identical to, censorship.

As electronic information resources become ever more available, librarians and information scientists have taken a strong stance that information equity is a central social responsibility. This means expanding library services to include Internet access and working to ensure that information is electronically accessible to all.

Social responsibility can have an affect on the employment policies of a library or information center; recent emphasis on providing opportunities for members of minority groups sometimes has resulted in preferential hiring practices. Here, too, there are conflicting arguments. One point of view is that such preference is only fair because for generations minorities (and women) were the targets of discrimination in many personnel practices and policies. The other view is that the preference itself is inappropriate and biased and that the only way to achieve fairness is to hire according to level of competence.

Opportunities in the Future

There are two major ways that a field can expand its opportunities: by enlarging the scope of its area of special competence and by demonstrating the need for more people to enter it.

Librarianship and the information sciences have been very successful in expanding the scope of their fields. For example, electronic resources are regularly administered by librarians who have developed the interest and skill to deal with them. The application of computer technology to most library operations has not only made services such as bibliographic searching and complicated interlibrary loans possible, but it has opened up the field so that individuals with computer science, management information systems (MIS), or systems analysis education are attracted to the profession. The field has grown by expanding its clientele. For example, improving the availability of information to business executives and that group's recognition of the value of good informational programs have been major factors in the development of many special libraries.

Effects of Society and Technology

Though it is always tempting to speculate about what information professionals may be doing in the future, it is important to keep in mind that—as always—librarianship will continue to be affected by society and technology. If, as some people predict, the school of the future will really be an individual workstation where a student connects to the Internet, it might seem that there will be no need for a librarian at the neighborhood school. However, imagine that there probably are several information professionals via the Internet at another location who are organizing the information the student receives. Their skills may be generally similar to those of today's school library media specialists.

Diversity of Opportunities

One long-range prediction seems safe: the diversity of opportunities available in librarianship and information science will continue. Though some specializations within the fields may not be required, the need for further specialization in other areas probably will increase the need for basic and continuing education. Increased specialization may limit the opportunities for individuals to move from one area of librarianship or information science to another. Those entering the field may need to decide their long-range areas of interest earlier than in the past. This can have an obvious effect on the educational programs in the fields, since the development of new specialties may send people back to school for further training.

Another factor is the success that librarians and information scientists may enjoy in the private sector. Though this part of the economy has traditionally employed only a small minority of librarians, if freelance opportunities are increased in number and if the special competencies of librarians and information scientists are used in more large industrial or commercial enterprises, the number of information professionals needed will also dramatically increase.

The Individual's Future

Most of us, however, are more concerned with our own individual futures, for the next ten or fifteen years, than we are with that of the profession as a whole. Some specializations, such as science librarians, systems administrators, or youth services librarians, continue to be in especially short supply.

If you are entering librarianship as a profession, you may be torn between trying to prepare in as general a way as possible to find a position and stressing your special background because it may be important to find the kind of position that best suits you. This creates a kind of tension that may cause you to miss some opportunities because your general background is comparable to that of many others who are seeking the same kind of opportunity. Some specialties may not be in urgent demand, so their value is therefore more limited.

The Nature of the Job

In some ways, examining the fields of librarianship and information science is like examining an elephant the way the legendary three blind men did. To the man at one end, the elephant was all tail; to the one in the middle, the elephant was like a wall; to the third, feeling the tusks had still a different impression. Information scientists who work in the management area of their field may be unaware of the skills needed in dealing with people—skills that are still needed by those in librarianship who are interpreting reference questions, explaining the use of the library, or testifying before the city council to persuade the public to support a library bond issue. A librarian working with children in a school library media center may wonder why he or she ever needed to master a foreign language or learn cataloging, while a colleague in the processing center of the same school system could not survive without those skills.

Planning, managing, supervising, and administering complex library systems are the work of librarians and information scientists, but these are still fields where there is room for people who want to be in an entrepreneurial role, too. Perhaps best of all is the fact that you may be able to move from one sort of specialty to another in the course of a career. The person who wants to continue in direct public service may do so, and another who aspires to major administrative responsibilities can move in that direction, while a third, perhaps with additional education acquired in the course of full-time work, can move into a new specialty.

Is It in Your Future?

If you are convinced that the information professions make up a field in which you can find personal and professional satisfaction, you will find a large variety of job opportunities. It is important for you to assess your own abilities, prepare yourself with the educational requirements, and use individuals in the field as touchstones, who may be able to advise you about possible opportunities that would be appropriate for you. What those individuals may not be knowledgeable about is the general outlook for positions. Because of this, you should review placement literature, noting which skills or specialties are among the most sought, and if the available positions are in the kinds of libraries and localities where you want to work. For those in the information professions, openness to experience, willingness to try new places to live or new kinds of specialties, commitment to librarianship, and personal qualities such as a sense of purpose and a certain toughness and interest in others—these qualities are as likely to be important in the future as they have been in the past.

Appendix A

Library and Information Science Professional Organizations

INDIVIDUALS WHO SHARE common interests and work naturally form organizations that may serve to exchange information, encourage education, and in general improve the status of those who make up its membership. Librarianship and information science have their share of these, with regional, state, national, and international groups. In some instances, large cities have their own clubs or chapters of some larger association.

Some directory information about various associations follows. Readers who wish a more thorough introduction to particular groups, including their founding date, their goals, and other details, may consult the latest edition of the *Encyclopedia of Associations*, a publication of Gale Research Corporation, or the *Bowker Annual Library and Book Trade Almanac*, a publication of R. R. Bowker. Readers should search the Internet to find additional organizations and information sources.

A letter or e-mail to each association asking for information on library and information science can bring you more data on specialized careers.

American Association for Artificial Intelligence
445 Burgess Dr.
Menlo Park, CA 94025
www.aaai.org

The American Association for Artificial Intelligence (AAAI) is a nonprofit scientific society devoted to advancing the scientific understanding of the mechanisms underlying thought and intelligent behavior and their embodiment in machines. AAAI aims to increase public understanding of artificial intelligence, improve the teaching and training of AI practitioners, and provide guidance for research planners and funders concerning the importance and potential of current AI developments and future directions.

American Association of Law Libraries
53 W. Jackson, Ste. 940
Chicago, IL 60604
www.washlaw.edu

American Indian Library Association
c/o Joan Howland Law Library
University of Minnesota
229 19th St., South
Minneapolis, MN 55455
www.aila.library.sd.gov

The American Indian Library Association is an affiliate of the American Library Association.

American Library Association (ALA)
50 E. Huron
Chicago, IL 60611
www.ala.org
and
615 New Hampshire Ave. NW, 1st Fl.
Washington, DC 20009
www.ala.org

The ALA provides opportunities for the professional development and education of librarians, library staff, and trustees. It promotes continuous, lifelong learning for all people through library and information services.

American Medical Informatics Association
4915 St. Elmo Ave., Ste. 401
Bethesda, MD 20814
www.amia.org

The American Medical Informatics Association's mission is to advance the field by fostering innovation and scientific exchange, educating professionals and the public, and influencing decision and policy makers regarding the use of information in health and biomedicine.

American Society for Information Science and Technology (ASIS)
1320 Fenwick La., Ste. 510
Silver Spring, MD 20910
www.asis.org

The American Society for Information Science and Technology (ASIS) provides education and networking opportunities to information professionals (including librarians, Web masters, information specialists, educators, researchers, publishers, information center managers) in organizations around the world. The ASIS bridges the gap between information science research and information services practice.

American Theological Library Association
300 S. Wacker Dr., Ste. 2100
Chicago, IL 60606
www.atla.com

Membership in the American Theological Library Association is open to any person engaged in professional library or bibliographic work in theological or religious fields or who has an interest in the literature of religion, theological librarianship, and the purposes and work of the association.

Art Libraries Society of North America
329 March Rd., Ste. 232
Ottawa, ON K2K 2E1
Canada
www.arlisna.org

Through its conferences, publications, awards, and website, the Art Libraries Society of North America provides resources and services for the worldwide arts information community.

Association of Canadian Archivists
P.O. Box 2596, Station D
Ottawa, ON K1P 5W6
Canada
archivists.ca/home

The Association of Canadian Archivists has a fourfold focus: 1. to provide leadership for everyone engaged in the preservation of Canada's documentary heritage; 2. to encourage awareness of archival activities and developments and the importance of archives to modern society; 3. to advocate the interests and needs of professional archivists before government and other regulatory agencies; and 4. to further the understanding and cooperation among members of the Canadian archival system and other information- and culture-based professions.

Association of Canadian Map Libraries and Archives
c/o Visual and Sound Archives Division
National Archives of Canada
395 Wellington St.
Ottawa, ON K1A 0N3
Canada
www.ssc.uwo.ca/assoc/acml/acmla.html

The Association of Canadian Map Libraries and Archives actively serves as the representative professional group for Canadian map librarians, cartographic archivists, and others interested in geographic information in all formats.

Association of Christian Librarians
P.O. Box 4
Cedarville, OH 45314
www.acl.org

The Association of Christian Librarians is an organization of evangelical Christian academic librarians that promotes the professional and spiritual growth of its members and provides service to the academic library community worldwide.

Association for Information and Image Management (AIIM)
AIIM International
1100 Wayne Ave., Ste. 1100
Silver Spring, MD 20910
www.aiim.org

The Association for Information and Image Management (AIIM)'s core focus is to connect users with suppliers who can help them apply document and content technologies to improve their internal processes.

Association for Information Systems (AIS)
AIS Administrative Office
P.O. Box 2712
Atlanta, GA 30301
www.aisnet.org

The Association for Information System (AIS)'s purpose is to serve academics specializing in information systems. Its mission is to advance knowledge of how the use of information technology can lead to improved organizational performance and individual quality of work life.

Association of Jewish Libraries
15 E. 26th St., Rm. 1034
New York, NY 10010
www.jewishlibraries.org

The Association of Jewish Libraries is dedicated to supporting the production, collection, organization, and dissemination of Judaic resources and library/media/information services in the United States, Canada, and more than twenty-three other countries.

Association of Research Libraries (ARL)
21 Dupont Circle, Ste. 800
Washington, DC 20036
arl.cni.org

ARL comprises the leading research libraries in North America. Its mission is to shape and influence forces affecting the future of research libraries in the process of scholarly communication. ARL programs and services promote equitable access to and effective use of recorded knowledge in support of teaching, research, scholarship, and community service.

Canadian Health Libraries Association
P.O. Box 94038
3324 Yonge St.
Toronto, ON M4N 3R1
Canada
www.med.mun.ca/chla

The Canadian Health Libraries Association's mission is to improve health/health care by promoting excellence in access to information.

Canadian Library Association
328 Frank St.
Ottawa, ON K2P 0X8
Canada
www.cla.ca

The Canadian Library Association provides services to a diverse group of individuals and organizations involved with or interested in library or information sciences.

CAUSE, The Association for the Management of Information Technology in Higher Education
4840 Pearl East Circle, Ste. 302E
Boulder, CO 80301
www.cni.org/docs/CAUSE.html

CAUSE's mission is to promote more effective planning, management, and evaluation of all information technologies in colleges and universities and to help individual member representatives develop as professionals in the field of higher education technology management.

International Association of Aquatic and Marine Science
    Libraries and Information Centers
c/o Library Harbor Branch Oceanographic Institution, Inc.
5600 US 1 North
Fort Pierce, FL 34946
www.iamslic.org

The International Association of Aquatic and Marine Science Libraries
and Information Centers is an association of individuals and organizations interested in aquatic and marine information science. The association provides a forum for exchange and exploration of ideas and
issues of mutual concern.

International Association of Music Information Centres
Stiftgasse 29, A-1070
Vienna, Austria
www.iamic.ie

The International Association of Music Information Centres is open
to the public and has extensive resources to offer. In addition to large
libraries of sheet music and sound archives, some centers maintain up-
to-date collections of biographical and research material, many issue
publications and recordings, and all of them serve as a focus of musical activity.

International Association of School Librarianship
Dept. 962, Box 34069
Seattle, WA 98124
www.hi.is/~anne/iasl.html

The International Association of School Librarianship's mission is to
provide an international forum for those interested in promoting effective school library media programs as viable instruments in the educational process.

International Association of Technological University Libraries
Dublin University Library
Dublin 9 Ireland
www.iatul.org

The International Association of Technological University Libraries was founded in Düsseldorf, Germany, in 1955, as an international forum for the exchange of ideas relevant to librarianship in technological universities throughout the world.

International Council on Archives
60 rue de Francs-Bourgeois
75003 Paris, France
www.ica.org

The International Council on Archives brings together national archive administrations, professional associations of archivists, regional and local archives, and archives of other organizations as well as individual archivists.

International Federation for Information Processing
Hofstraße 3
A-2361 Laxenburg, Austria
www.ifip.or.at

The International Federation for Information Processing is a nongovernmental, nonprofit umbrella organization for national societies working in the field of information processing.

International Federation for Systems Research
www.ifsr.org

The main purpose of the International Federation for Systems Research is to advance cybernetic and systems research and systems applications and to serve the international systems community.

Medical Library Association
65 E. Wacker Pl., Ste. 1900
Chicago, IL 60602
www.mlahq.org

The Medical Library Association is dedicated to improving the quality and leadership of the health information professional to foster the art and science of health information services.

Music Library Association
6707 Old Dominion Dr., Ste. 315
McLean, VA 22101
www.musiclibraryassoc.org

The Music Library Association is the professional organization in the United States devoted to music librarianship and to all aspects of music materials in libraries.

National Association of Government Archives and Records
    Administrators
c/o AMR Management Services
201 E. Main St., Ste. 1405
Lexington, KY 40507
nascio.org

The National Association of Government Archives and Records Administrators represents state chief information officers and information technology executives and managers from state governments across the United States.

National Association of State Information Resource Executives
167 W. Main St., Ste. 600
Lexington, KY 40507
www.nasire.org

The National Association of State Information Resource Executives represents state chief information officers and information resource executives and managers from the fifty states, six United States territories, and the District of Columbia.

Progressive Librarians Guild
P.O. Box 2203, Times Square Station
New York, NY 10108
libr.org/PLG

The Progressive Librarians Guild is committed to providing a forum for the open exchange of radical views on library issues; conducting campaigns to support progressive and democratic library activities locally, nationally, and internationally; supporting activist librarians as they work to effect changes in their own libraries and communities; and bridging the artificial and destructive gaps between school, public, academic, and special libraries and between public and technical services.

Public Library Association (PLA)
50 E. Huron St.
Chicago, IL 60611
www.pla.org

The PLA's purpose is to advance the development and effectiveness of public library service and public librarians.

REFORMA, The National Association to Promote Library Services to the Spanish Speaking
P.O. Box 4386
Fresno, CA 93744
www.reforma.org

REFORMA is committed to the improvement of the full spectrum of library and information services for the approximately thirty million Spanish-speaking and Latino people in the United States.

Society of American Archivists
527 S. Wells St., 5th Fl.
Chicago, IL 60607
www.archivists.org

Society of American Archivists membership is open to those who are or have been engaged in the custody or control of records, archives, or private papers or who wish to support the objectives of the society.

Special Libraries Association
1700 Eighteenth St. NW
Washington, DC 20009
www.sla.org

The Special Libraries Association's mission is to advance the leadership role of its members in putting knowledge to work for the benefit of decision makers in corporations, government, the professions, and society. It shapes the destiny of our information and knowledge-based society.

A list of this kind only suggests the diversity of interests represented by the larger associations. Most of these groups have sections, divisions, or chapters—smaller groups that are concerned with one area of specialization or one geographic region. Library and information sciences associations are listed in the *Bowker Annual Library and Book Trade Almanac* and on the Internet.

Appendix B

Educational Programs in Librarianship and Information Science

THE NUMBER AND variety of educational programs in librarianship and information science can confuse you when considering whether to enroll in a program of professional or technical education in one of these areas. Though local institutions may offer programs, you should get a sense of what the range of opportunity is and learn as much as possible about the various programs in operation at different institutions. Sometimes, career counseling offices or libraries provide catalogs from the different educational programs. However, some directory assistance is necessary to provide addresses of programs so you can write for more information. The directories are usually in the process of revision. Always use the latest edition since its information is most current.

The American Library Association Standing Committee on Library Education is the best central source for information on different levels of library and information science education. For the items in the bulleted list below, contact:

American Library Association
Standing Committee on Library Education
50 E. Huron St.
Chicago, IL 60611
www.ala.org

- Guidelines for choosing a library and information studies graduate program
- Financial assistance for library education
- Requirements for admission and a degree
- Joint degrees offered by library education programs
- Information about graduate library education programs
- Library technical assistant programs
- Undergraduate programs in library education
- Graduate library education programs (which are revised semiannually)

The last bulleted item lists masters, advanced study, as well as doctoral-level programs in both the United States and Canada. Because study in an accredited program of library and information science is the most common way to gain the professional credentials needed for information work, the accredited programs and their addresses are provided here. Contact schools in which you are interested for complete information on the course of study and financial aid opportunities.

United States

Alabama

The University of Alabama
School of Library and Information Studies
Box 870252
Tuscaloosa, AL 35487
www.slis.ua.edu
Master of library and information studies
Distance education opportunities

Arizona

University of Arizona
School of Information Resources and Library Science
1515 E. First St.
Tucson, AZ 85719
www.sir.arizona.edu
Master of arts
Distance education opportunities on the Internet

California

San Jose State University
School of Library and Information Sciences
One Washington Sq.
San Jose, CA 95192
www.slisweb.sjsu.edu
Master of library and information science
Distance education opportunities
Web-supported programs with two-way interactive video

University of California–Los Angeles
Department of Information Studies
Graduate School of Education and Information Studies
2320 Moore Hall, Mailbox 951521
Los Angeles, CA 90095
is.gseis.ucla.edu
Master of library and information science

Colorado

See Kansas, Emporia State University

Connecticut

Southern Connecticut State University
School of Communication, Information, and Library Science
Department of Library Science and Instructional Technology
501 Crescent St.
New Haven, CT 06515
www.SouthernCT.edu/~brownm
Master of library science
Distance education opportunities for online MLS

District of Columbia

The Catholic University of America
School of Library and Information Science
620 Michigan Ave. NE
Washington, DC 20064
www.cua.edu
Master of science in library information
Distance education opportunities

Florida

Florida State University
School of Information Studies
Tallahassee, FL 32306
www.fsu.edu/~lis
Master of science, master of arts
Distance education opportunities on the Internet

University of South Florida
School of Library and Information Science
4202 E. Fowler Ave., CIS 1040
Tampa, FL 33620
www.cas.usf.edu/lis
Master of arts
Distance education opportunities and on the Internet

Georgia

Clark Atlanta University
School of Library and Information Studies
300 Trevor Arnett Hall
223 James P. Brawley Dr.
Atlanta, GA 30314
www.cau.edu
Master of science in library service

Hawaii

University of Hawaii
Library and Information Science Program
2550 The Mall
Honolulu, HI 96822
www.hawaii.edu/slis
Master of library and information science
Distance education opportunities for Hawaii Interactive Television
   System limited to the islands

Illinois

Dominican University
Graduate School of Library and Information Science
7900 W. Division St.
River Forest, IL 60305
www.dom.edu/academic/gslishome.html
www.stkate.edu (College of St. Catherine)
Master of library and information science
Distance education opportunities

University of Illinois at Urbana–Champaign
Graduate School of Library and Information Science
Library and Information Science Bldg.
501 E. Daniel St.
Champaign, IL 61820
www.alexia.lis.uiuc.edu
Master of science
Distance education opportunities on the Internet

Indiana

Indiana University
School of Library and Information Science
Main Library 012
1320 E. Tenth St.
Bloomington, IN 47405
www.slis.indiana.edu
Master of library science, master of information science

Iowa

University of Iowa
School of Library and Information Science
3087 Library
The University of Iowa
Iowa City, IA 52242
www.uiowa.edu/~libsci
Master of arts
Distance education opportunities

Kansas

Emporia State University
School of Library and Information Management
P.O. Box 4025
Emporia, KS 66801
www.slim.emporia.edu
Master of library science
Distance education opportunities
Videotape, statewide teleconferencing system, and Internet usage

Kentucky

University of Kentucky
College of Communications and Information Studies
School of Library and Information Science
502 King Library Bldg. S
Lexington, KY 40506
www.uky.edu/CommInfoStudies/SLIS
Master of arts, master of science in library science
Distance education opportunities
Interactive video and Internet usage

Louisiana

Louisiana State University
School of Library and Information Science
267 Coates Hall
Baton Rouge, LA 70803
www.slis.lsu.edu
Master of library and information science
Distance education opportunities
Two-way interactive video and the Internet (selected courses)

Maine

See South Carolina, University of South Carolina

Maryland

University of Maryland
College of Information Studies
4105 Hornbake Library Bldg.
College Park, MD 20742
www.clis.umd.edu
Master of library science

Massachusetts

Simmons College
Graduate School of Library and Information Science
300 The Fenway
Boston, MA 02115
www.simmons.edu/programs/gslis
Master of science

See also Rhode Island, University of Rhode Island

Michigan

University of Michigan
School of Information
304 W. Hall Bldg.
550 E. University Ave.
Ann Arbor, MI 48109
www.si.umich.edu
Master of science in information

Wayne State University
Library and Information Science Program
106 Kresge Library
Detroit, MI 48202
www.lisp.wayne.edu
Master of library and information science
Distance education opportunities

Minnesota

See Illinois, Dominican University; Texas, University of North Texas

Mississippi

University of Southern Mississippi
School of Library and Information Science
Box 5146
Hattiesburg, MS 39406
www-dept.usm.edu/~slis
Master of library and information science
Distance education opportunities, interactive video sites and on the
Internet, whole and partial online courses

Missouri

University of Missouri–Columbia
School of Information Science and Learning Technologies
303 Townsend Hall
Columbia, MO 65211
www.coe.missouri.edu/~sislt
Master of arts
Distance education opportunities and on the Internet

Nebraska

See Kansas, Emporia State University

New Hampshire

See Rhode Island, University of Rhode Island

New Jersey

Rutgers University
School of Communication, Information, and Library Studies
4 Huntington St.
New Brunswick, NJ 08901
www.scils.rutgers.edu
Master of library service

New Mexico

See Kansas, Emporia State University

New York

Long Island University
Palmer School of Library and Information Science
C. W. Post Campus
720 Northern Blvd.
Brookville, NY 11548
www.liu.edu/palmer
Master of science in library and information science
Distance education opportunities

Pratt Institute
School of Information and Library Science
Information Science Center
200 Willoughby Ave.
Brooklyn, NY 11205
www.sils.pratt.edu
Master of science in library and information science

Queens College
City University of New York
Graduate School of Library and Information Studies
65-30 Kissena Blvd.
Flushing, NY 11367
www.qc.edu/GSLIS
Master of library science

St. Johns University
Division of Library and Information Science
8000 Utopia Pkwy.
Jamaica, NY 11439
www.stjohns.edu/academics
Master of library science

Syracuse University
School of Information Studies
4-206 Center for Science and Technology
Syracuse, NY 13244
www.istweb.syr.edu
Master of library science
Distance education opportunities depending on desired degree,
    short one-week residencies for core courses, Internet-based home
    study for course assignment completion

University at Albany
State University of New York
School of Information Science and Policy
135 Western Ave., Drawer 113
Albany, NY 12222
www.albany.edu/dis
Master of library science
Distance education opportunities

University at Buffalo
State University of New York
Department of Library and Information Studies
534 Baldy Hall
Buffalo, NY 14260
www.gse.buffalo.edu/programs/lis
Master of library science
Distance education opportunities in Rochester (selected courses)
    and on the Internet (selected courses), two-way interactive video
    to Elmira (selected courses)

North Carolina

North Carolina Central University
School of Library and Information Sciences
1801 Fayetteville St.
P.O. Box 19586
Durham, NC 27707
www.nccu.edu/academics
Master of library science
Distance education opportunities

University of North Carolina–Chapel Hill
School of Information and Library Science
CB #3360, 100 Manning Hall
Chapel Hill, NC 27599
http://sils.unc.edu
Master of science in library science, master of science in
information science

The University of North Carolina at Greensboro
Department of Library and Information Studies
School of Education
P.O. Box 26171
Greensboro, NC 27402
www.uncg.edu/lis
Master of library and information studies
Distance education opportunities

Ohio

Kent State University
School of Library and Information Science
Rm. 314 Library
P.O. Box 5190
Kent, OH 44242
www.slis.kent.edu
Master of library and information science
Distance education opportunities

Oklahoma

University of Oklahoma
School of Library and Information Studies
401 W. Brooks, Rm. 120
Norman, OK 73019
www.ou.edu/cas/slis
Master of library and information studies
Distance education opportunities

Oregon

See Kansas, Emporia State University

Pennsylvania

Clarion University of Pennsylvania
Department of Library Science
840 Wood St.
Clarion, PA 16214
www.clarion.edu/libsci
Master of science in library science
Distance education opportunities, on-site or interactive television

Drexel University
College of Information Science and Technology
3141 Chestnut St.
Philadelphia, PA 19104
www.cis.drexel.edu
Master of science in library and information science
Distance education opportunities on the Internet

University of Pittsburgh
School of Information Sciences
505 IS Bldg.
Pittsburgh, PA 15260
www2.sis.pitt.edu
Master of library and information science

Puerto Rico

University of Puerto Rico
Graduate School of Information Sciences and Technologies
P.O. Box 21906
San Juan, PR 00931
www.upr.edu
Master of information sciences

Rhode Island

University of Rhode Island
Graduate School of Library and Information Studies
Rodman Hall
Kingston, RI 02881
www.uri.edu/artsci/lsc
Master of library and information studies
Distance education opportunities, Internet and interactive video
  usage

South Carolina

University of South Carolina
College of Library and Information Science
Davis College
Columbia, SC 29208
www.libsci.sc.edu
Master of library and information science
Distance education opportunities for degree programs in selected
  states per contract arrangements

Tennessee

University of Tennessee
School of Information Sciences
804 Volunteer Blvd.
Knoxville, TN 37996
www.sis.utk.edu
Master of science
Distance education opportunities

Texas

Texas Woman's University
School of Library and Information Studies
P.O. Box 425438
Denton, TX 76204
www.twu.edu/cope/slis/programs/masters.htm
Master of library science and master of arts in library science
Distance education opportunities, selected courses on the Internet

University of North Texas
School of Library and Information Sciences
P.O. Box 311068, NT Station
Denton, TX 76203
www.unt.edu/slis
Master of science
Distance education opportunities

The University of Texas at Austin
Graduate School of Library and Information Science
Sanchez Bldg. (SZB) 564
1 University Station D7000
Austin, TX 78712
www.gslis.utexas.edu
Master of library and information science
Distance education opportunities and interactive television

Utah

See Kansas, Emporia State University

Virginia

See District of Columbia, The Catholic University of America

Washington

University of Washington
The Information School
Mary Gates Hall, Ste. 370
Box 352840
Seattle, WA 98195
www.ischool.washington.edu
Master of library and information science
Distance education opportunities (through the continuing library
    education specialist at the UW extension office)

Wisconsin

University of Wisconsin–Madison
School of Library and Information Studies
Helen C. White Hall
600 N. Park St., Rm. 4217
Madison, WI 53706
www.slis.wisc.edu
Master of arts
Distance education opportunities ETN and Web-based

University of Wisconsin–Milwaukee
School of Library and Information Science
Enderis Hall 1110
2400 E. Hartford Ave.
Milwaukee, WI 53201
www.uwm.edu/Dept/SOIS
Master of library and information science
Distance education opportunities, satellite sites throughout
    Wisconsin, Internet usage

Canada

Alberta

University of Alberta
School of Library and Information Studies
3-20 Rutherford South
Edmonton, AB T6G 2J4
www.slis.ualberta.ca
Master of library and information studies

British Columbia

University of British Columbia
School of Library, Archival, and Information Studies
1956 Main Mall, Rm. 831
Vancouver, BC V6T 1Z1
www.slais.ubc.ca
Master of library and information studies

Nova Scotia

Dalhousie University
School of Library and Information Studies
Faculty of Management
Halifax, NS B3H 3J5
www.mgmt.dal.ca
Master of library and information studies

Ontario

University of Toronto
Faculty of Information Studies
140 St. George St.
Toronto, ON M5S 3G6
www.fis.utoronto.ca
Master of information studies
Distance education opportunities through videoconferencing and
the Internet

See also New York, Syracuse University

University of Western Ontario
Graduate Programs in Library and Information Science
Faculty of Information and Media Studies
Middlesex College
London, ON N6A 5B7
www.fims.uwo.ca/lis
Master of library and information science

Quebec

McGill University
Graduate School of Library and Information Studies
3459 McTavish St.
Montreal, QB H3A 1Y1
www.mcgill.ca/sis
Master of library and information studies

Université de Montréal
École de bibliothéconomie et des sciences de l'information
C.P. 6128, Succursale Centre-Ville
Montréal, QC H3C 3J7
www.ebsi.umontreal.ca
Maîtrise en sciences de l'information

SUGGESTED READING

THIS BOOK PROVIDES career information for those interested in librarianship or information science. Reading publications intended for students and those working in the field will provide even more. The many concerns and specializations within the library and information fields are reflected in and often shaped by the journals serving those areas. A review of any of these periodicals will provide ideas about current trends, major personalities, and general reports on the state of different parts of these career fields.

An alphabetical list of the various newsletters, magazines, and journals published within the American Library Association (ALA), including those available only over the Internet, follows. A brief profile is offered for each title, including the publishing frequency per year and availability of an online version. To order any of these periodicals, visit the ALA website at www.ala.org/ala/alalibrary/ala periodicals/alaperiodicals.cfm or contact the American Library Association, 50 East Huron Street, Chicago, IL 60611.

ALA Washington News—Available through ALA Washington office. Published at irregular intervals. Available free online at www.ala.org/ala/washoff/washoffnews/news.cfm.

ALCTS Newsletter Online—Association for Library Collections and Technical Services. Published online six times a year. See www.ala.org/ala/alcts/alcts.cfm.

ALSConnect Newsletter—Association for Library Service to Children. Published quarterly. Sent to ALSC members as part of membership. Unavailable by subscription.

American Libraries—The magazine of the American Library Association (ALA). Published ten times a year. Sent to ALA members as part of membership. *American Libraries* is available to libraries and other institutions by paid subscription. Online companion available at www.ala.org/ala/alonline/index.cfm.

baseline—An official publication of the American Library Association's Map and Geography Round Table (MAGERT). Published six times a year. Sent to MAGERT members as part of membership. Available by subscription: *baseline* Production Manager, Maps Library, Missouri State University, 901 South National, #175, Springfield, MO 65804. Issues available online at www.ala.org/ala/magert/publicationsab/Publicationsa.htm.

Book Links: Connecting Books, Libraries, and Classrooms—Magazine published by Booklist Publications, an imprint of the American Library Association. Published bimonthly. Available by subscription: Book Links, Subscription Department, American Library Association, 50 E. Huron St., Chicago, IL 60611. Online version available at www.ala.org/BookLinks.

Booklist—Magazine published by Booklist Publications, an imprint of the American Library Association. Includes reference books bulletin. Published bimonthly September through June and monthly in July and August. Available by subscription. Online companion available at the *Booklist* home page at www.ala.org/ala/BookLinks.

CHOICE: Current Reviews for Academic Libraries—Association of College and Research Libraries. Published monthly except bimonthly in July/August. Available by subscription: Subscriptions, CHOICE, 100 Riverview Center, Middletown, CT 06457. For online subscription: www.ala.org/ala/acrl/acrlpubs/choice/howtoorder/howto order.cfm. Online companion available at the CHOICE home page at www.ala.org/acrl/choice/home.html.

CLENExchange—Official publication of the Continuing Library Education Network and Exchange Round Table (CLENERT). Published quarterly. Sent to CLENERT members as part of membership. Available by subscription: ALA/CLENERT, 50 E. Huron St., Chicago, IL 60611. Available free online at www.ala.org/alaorg/rtables/clene/ clenexchange.html.

College and Research Libraries—Official journal of the Association of College and Research Libraries (ACRL). Published bimonthly. Sent to all ACRL members as part of membership. Available by subscription: College and Research Libraries, Subscription Department, c/o CHOICE, 100 Riverview Center, Middletown, CT 06457. Online companion available at www.ala.org/ala/acrl/acrlpubs/crljournal/ collegeresearch.cfm. Online subscription at www.ala.org/ala/ acrl/acrlpubs/choice/howtoorder/offlineorder.cfm.

College and Research Libraries News—Association of College and
   Research Libraries (ACRL). Published monthly except
   bimonthly July/August issue. Sent to all ACRL members as
   part of membership. Available by subscription: C&RL News,
   c/o CHOICE Subscriptions, 100 Riverview Center,
   Middletown, CT 06457. Online companion available at
   www.ala.org/ala/acrl/acrlpubs/crlnews/collegeresearch.cfm.
   Online subscription at www.ala.org/ala/acrl/acrlpubs/choice/
   howtoorder/offlineorder.cfm.

Counterpoise: For Social Responsibilities, Liberty and Dissent—
   Alternative review journal published by the Alternatives in
   Print Task Force of the Social Responsibilities Round Table.
   Published quarterly. Available by subscription only:
   Counterpoise, 1716 SW Williston Rd., Gainesville, FL
   32608. Online companion available at counterpoise.info/
   intern2.asp. For online subscription, counterpoise.info/
   subscribe5.asp.

Documents to the People—Official publication of the Government
   Documents Round Table (GODORT). Published quarterly.
   Sent annually to GODORT members as part of membership.
   Available by subscription: Documents Librarian, University
   Library, 801 S. Morgan St., M/C 234, University of Illinois,
   Chicago, IL 60607. Information available online at
   www.ala.org/ala/godort/dttp/dttponline/ Default6913.htm.

EMIE Bulletin—Ethnic and Multicultural Information Exchange
   Round Table (EMIERT). Published quarterly. Sent to
   EMIERT members as part of membership. Available by
   subscription: Publisher, EMIE Bulletin, Queens College,
   Graduate School of Library and Information Studies, 65-30
   Kissena Blvd., Flushing, New York 11367.

Federal Librarian—Federal Librarians Round Table (FLRT).
Published four times a year. Sent to FFLRT members as part
of membership. Available by subscription. Information
available online at www.ala.org/ala/faflrt/faflrtnewsletter/
newsletter.cfm.

Footnotes—New Members Round Table (NMRT). Published four
times a year in August, November, February, and May. Sent to
NMRT members as part of membership. Available online at
www.ala.org/ala/nmrt/footnotes/index.htm.

GLBTRT Newsletter—Gay, Lesbian, Bisexual, and Transgendered
Round Table (GLBTRT). Published quarterly. Available to
GLBTRT members as part of membership. Information
available online at isd.usc.edu/~trimmer/glbtrt/
newsletter.htm.

IFRT Report—Intellectual Freedom Round Table (IFRT). Online
version published twice per year. Sent to IFRT members as
part of membership. Available online at www.nd.cdu/
~jarcher/ifrtreport/home.html.

Information Technology and Libraries—Library and Information
Technology Association (LITA). Published quarterly. Sent to
LITA members as part of membership. Available by
subscription: Information Technology and Libraries,
Subscription Department, American Library Association, 50
E. Huron St., Chicago, IL 60611. Online companion
available at Information Technology and Libraries at
www.lita.org/ala/lita/litapublications/ital/italinformation.cfm.

Interface—Official publication of the Association of Specialized
and Cooperative Library Agencies (ASCLA). Published
quarterly. Sent to ASCLA members as part of membership.
Available by subscription: Interface, American Library

Association, 50 E. Huron St., Chicago, IL 60611. Online companion available at the ASCLA Publications.

International Leads—Official publication of the International Relations Round Table (IRRT). Published quarterly. Sent to IRRT members as part of membership. Available by subscription: International Relations Office, American Library Association, 50 E. Huron St., Chicago, IL 60611. Online companion available at International Relations Round Table at www.ala.org/ala/irrt/intlleads/international.cfm.

Knowledge Quest—An official journal of the American Association of School Librarians (AASL). Published bimonthly September through May (five issues per year). Sent to AASL members as part of membership. Available by subscription: Knowledge Quest, Subscription Department, American Library Association, 50 E. Huron St., Chicago, IL 60611. Online companion available at www.ala.org/ala/aasl/aaslpubsandjournals/kqweb/kqweb.cfm.

Library Administration and Management—Official journal of the Library Administration and Management Association (LAMA). Published quarterly. Sent to LAMA members as part of membership. Available by subscription: Library Administration and Management, Subscription Department, American Library Association, 50 E. Huron St., Chicago, IL 60611. Online companion available at www.ala.org/ala/lama/lamapublications/laandm/lamhome/lamonline.cfm.

Library History Round Table Newsletter—Library History Round Table (LHRT). Published semiannually. Sent to LHRT members as part of membership. Unavailable by subscription.

Online companion at www.ala.org/ala/lhrt/lhrtnewsletters/
lhrtnewsletters.cfm.

Library Instruction Round Table News—Library Instruction
Round Table (LIRT). Published quarterly. Sent to LIRT
members as part of membership. Unavailable by subscription.
Online companion at www3.baylor.edu/LIRT/lirtnews.

Library Resources and Technical Services—Official journal of the
Association for Library Collections and Technical Services
(ALCTS). Published quarterly. Sent to all ALCTS members as
part of membership. Available by subscription: Library
Resources and Technical Services, Subscription Department,
American Library Association, 50 E. Huron St., Chicago, IL
60611. Online companion at LRTS online at
www.ala.org/alcts/lrts.

Library Technology Reports—Journal published by ALA
TechSource, an imprint of the American Library Association
(ALA). Published bimonthly. Available by subscription only:
Circulation Manager, Library Technology Reports, ALA
TechSource, 50 E. Huron St., Chicago, IL 60611.
Information, including cumulative index, available online at
www.techsource.ala.org/ltr.

Newsletter on Intellectual Freedom—Office for Intellectual
Freedom (OIF). Published bimonthly (January, March, May,
July, September, November). Available by subscription only:
Newsletter on Intellectual Freedom, Subscription
Department, American Library Association, 50 E. Huron St.,
Chicago, IL 60611. Information available online for
Newsletter on Intellectual Freedom at members.ala.org/nif/
archives/archives.html.

Prism—Office for Accreditation. Published quarterly. See
   www.ala.org/ala/accreditation/prp/prism/current/onepage1/
   everythingissue.cfm.

Public Libraries—Official journal of the Public Library
   Association (PLA). Published bimonthly. Sent to PLA
   members as part of membership. Available by subscription:
   Public Libraries, Subscription Department, American Library
   Association, 50 E. Huron St., Chicago, IL 60611. Online
   companion available at www.ala.org/ala/pla/plapubs/
   publiclibraries/publiclibraries.cfm.

*RBM: A Journal of Rare Books, Manuscripts, and Cultural
   Heritage*—Association of College and Research Libraries
   (ACRL). Published twice a year. RBM is an independent
   ACRL publication. Sent to members and nonmembers of
   ACRL's Rare Books and Manuscripts Section only with
   subscription order to: CHOICE/ACRL Subscriptions, P.O.
   Box 141, Annapolis Junction, MD 20701. Information
   available online at www.ala.org/ala/acrl/acrlpubs/rbm/
   rbm.cfm.

Reference Books Bulletin—Published in *Booklist*. Online
   companion available at *Reference Books Bulletin* at
   www.ala.org/booklist.

Reference and User Services Quarterly—Official publication of the
   Reference and User Services Association (RUSA). Sent to
   RUSA members as part of membership. Available by
   subscription: Reference and User Services Quarterly,
   Subscription Department, American Library Association,
   50 E. Huron St., Chicago, IL 60611. Online companion
   available at www.rusq.org.

RUSA Update—Official newsletter of the Reference and User Services Association (RUSA). Published quarterly. Sent to RUSA members as part of membership. Available by subscription: RUSA Update, 50 E. Huron St., Chicago, IL 60611. Online companion available as part of RUSA at www.rusa.org.

School Library Media Research—An official journal of the American Association of School Librarians. Published online only. See www.ala.org/ala/aasl/aaslpubsandjournals/slmrb/schoollibrary.cfm.

Smart Libraries Newsletter (formerly *Library Systems Newsletter*)—Published by ALA TechSource, an imprint of the American Library Association (ALA). Published monthly. Available by subscription only: Circulation Manager, Library Systems Newsletter, ALA TechSource, 50 E. Huron St., Chicago, IL 60611. Information, including a sample issue, available online at www.techsource.ala.org/sln.

SORT Bulletin—Staff Organizations Round Table (SORT). Published semiannually. Sent to SORT members as part of membership. Unavailable by subscription. For more information, www.ala.org/ala/sort/sortpublications/sortbulletin/sortbulletin.htm.

SRRT Newsletter—Social Responsibilities Round Table (SRRT). Published quarterly. Sent to SRRT members as part of membership. Available by subscription: SRRT Newsletter, American Library Association, 50 E. Huron St., Chicago, IL 60611. See http://libr.org/srrt/docs.

The Voice—Association for Library Trustees and Advocates (ALTA). Published quarterly. Sent to ALTA members as part

of membership. Unavailable by subscription. Issues online at
www.ala.org/ala/alta/altapubssubs.

Women in Libraries—Feminist Task Force of the Social
Responsibilities Round Table (SRRT). Published quarterly.
Available by subscription only—$5 per year: Publisher,
Women in Libraries, c/o ALA, 50 E. Huron St., Chicago, IL
60611. Selected articles available online at www.libr.org/
ftf/WIL/wil.html.